"Becoming a New York doorman opened many doors for me."

—ESTEBAN PLOTKY, FORMER DICTATOR
NOW DOORMAN FIRST CLASS,
EMBASSY PALACE TOWERS

"IT BECAME MY PRIVILEGE TO SERVE THE PRIVILEGED"

I'LL TAKE CARE OF THAT, MRS. FINE!

"I MARCHED IN THE DOORMAN'S PRIDE DAY PARADE ON FABULOUS FIFTH AVENUE"

Doorman Proud!

"BUILDING MANAGEMENT BESTOWED MEDALS AND COCKADES UPON ME"

"THE HOLIDAY SEASON— ALWAYS A SPECIAL TIME FOR ME"

I CAN'T EAT CHEESE LOGS.

"I WAS READY TO STEP UP IN ANY EMERGENCY"

OH, ESTEBAN, HELP! MY ZIP IS STUCK.

"IT FELT GOOD MENTORING POOR KIDS AT THE DOORMEN OF TOMORROW CAMP"

REMEMBER — YOU'RE WORKING FOR TIPS.

TAXI?

"Join me in the ranks of New York's Politest!"

BY MICHAEL GERBER

WELCOME TO THE BIG CITY, KID

I still love New York, God knows why.

Like most catastrophes, *The Bull Street Journal* started out as a pretty good idea. It was late 1995, and I'd just moved back to New York from Seattle, turning down a job at a startup called Amazon (weird name!) to get a master's in publishing at NYU. This was not the pretty good idea; this was the terrible idea. A literary career is always a terrible idea, but picking one over Amazon in 1995? And paying twenty grand for the privilege? *Jesus Christ.*

On the other hand, being back in New York had reconnected me with Jon Schwarz, my dear friend from *The Yale Record.* Aunt Sallie Mae had sprung for a tiny studio apartment in the West Village, and an even tinier cat named Fifi. As my last borrowed $100's burned, I became that quintessential New York type: a young man on the make. I was hot for an idea, any idea, that would make a splash, make my name, and make me and Fifi a big pile of money.

I was sitting in the Reading Room of the NYPL when I found it. In 1982, some folks (including a few *Bystanders*) had created a parody of *The Wall Street Journal. Off the Wall Street Journal* had sold 350,000 copies, and its sequel 250,000 more. From my college days, I knew newspaper parodies could be cash cows; they were cheap to print, and newsstands would front you the money once you showed them a prototype, which I could make on my Mac. And in the 14 years since '82, the *WSJ* had become *the* national organ of conservatism, an even fatter, worthier target.

MICHAEL GERBER

(@mgerber937) is Editor & Publisher of *The American Bystander.*

The Bull Street Journal seemed like a slam dunk, and Jon and I tore into it. I would sit at my computer for hours on end, Jon pacing behind me throwing out jokes. Jon's high school friend Rob Weisberg would drop by with writing, and illustrators Todd Lynch and Cullum Rogers mailed in excellent art. Production took place at the old Kinko's on Astor Place, late at night when you could walk out without paying, not that we ever did that (we did that constantly).

When the 100-copy test print came back, all broadsheet and beautiful, Jon, Rob and I went out onto the stoop. We sat in the golden spring dusk, smoking a few nice cigars I'd squirrelled away, handing out copies to my neighbors. We could hear laughter from the open windows above; it was a hit. The next day, brimming with hope, I sent *The Bull Street Journal* to a handful of editors.

Within 72 hours, a book editor at HarperCollins had called. "Who are you guys?" he asked, a question we'd hear a lot. By the time I'd hung up, he'd made a preliminary offer of $100,000.

"This is just a prototype," I said. "We want to spruce up the art, and match the typefaces exactly."

"Cool, cool," he said. "We're meeting Friday. I'm 95% sure we'll get this done."

Friday morning he called. "One last question: how do we package it?"

I'd been expecting this. "Quarterfold it, put a stiff cardboard U-shaped picture wrap around it, and shrinkwrap," I said. "That way you can put it on newsstands, or sell it on bookstore shelves for longer, at a higher price."

"What a great idea!" the book editor said. "That's how you get to be a rich man. I'll be in touch."

He wasn't. Finally, the letter came. It began, "Unfortunately…" The rest didn't matter.

We hardly even noticed; in the meantime we'd been contacted by the editor of a highly respected literary journal.

"Who are you guys?" he said. "I loved this thing. I read every goddamn word."

Jon and I stammered out a thank you; in those pre-Remnick years, his magazine was by far the smartest thing in print. I especially liked his essays, which always seemed to mix current affairs with weird bits of Roman history. "The phenomenon of the Furby calls to mind Tiberius and Gaius Gracchus…"

"Can you guys have lunch tomorrow?" he asked. "I really want to move on this."

The next day, over club sandwiches at The Yale Club, turkey was talked. "So, how much do you want?"

Jon and I looked at each other. "What do you think would be fair?"

The editor laughed. "Never say that to someone in publishing." He was utterly charming, one of his columns brought to life, brilliant, a little rascally, impeccably dressed. Jon and I liked him immensely.

I swallowed. "Well, HarperCollins made a soft offer of a hundred grand."

The editor didn't flinch. "Seems about right," he said. "It's a good time for this—people are so sick of Wall Street bullshit. This parody is more than funny, it's important."

We, naturally, agreed.

"We're going to put this on every goddamn newsstand in the country," the editor said as we walked down the stairs to the lobby, his words echoing off the stones. "So we've got a deal?"

The editor offered his hand, and we shook it. "Call my office first thing tomorrow morning, and we'll get the lawyers drawing up the contract."

As Jon and I watched him walk out of the Club, we were giddy. The New York dream. It was all about to happen.

The next morning, I called the editor's office. "My name is Michael Gerber, I'm calling for [editor's name]."

"One moment," a woman said. It was a long moment. Then: "Can you tell me what this is regarding?"

"We wrote a parody of *The Wall Street Journal* which he really liked—"

Jon, ever-pacing, stopped. I kept talking.

"—actually he *loved* it. He says the magazine wants to publish it. We had lunch with him yesterday and—"

The assistant cut me off. "I see. One moment."

This moment was, impossibly, even longer than the first one. Finally she returned. "Mr. [name] has no idea what you're talking about."

"That's impossible," I said. "We talked with him for three hours."

"That's as may be, but—"

"We actually shook hands on a deal, lady!"

Her tone, never friendly, grew icy. "Sir, he has no idea what you're talking about, and doesn't want to talk to you."

"Okay," I said, utterly confused, trying to keep my composure. "Is there anyone else—the publisher, maybe, who—"

"No," she said firmly.

"But if I could just—"

She hung up.

I put down the phone.

"My god, what just happened?"

"He didn't remember us."

"*Didn't remember*?" Jon grabbed the phone. "She must've made a mistake. I'm calling."

I practically slapped the receiver out of Jon's hand. "Don't."

"Are you crazy?"

"I grew up with people like this," I said. "He was drunk. Either he won't remember, or you'll make him remember, and he'll hate you for it. We can't afford to make such a powerful enemy."

Slowly Jon relented. "I'll tell you this," he said. "I'm cancelling my fucking subscription to [highly respected journal]!"

We didn't have time to mope. A few days after that, I heard from another secretary. "Hello, I'm calling from Curt MacGruber's office. He was very impressed with your project and would like to talk with you about it tomorrow at two. Would that work?"

"Absolutely," I said, and spent the next 24 hours researching the man. "Before becoming the publisher of America's biggest rock and roll magazine, MacGruber started in politics. He was deeply involved with McGovern in '72," I read to Jon over the phone. Jon had been so shook up by the earlier call, I'd handle this one myself, and call after with what would surely be good news.

I called at 1:57; back in those days, I was early for things. "Mr. MacGruber has been waiting for you, please hold."

The phone picked up abruptly, and a brash, abrasive voice began. "You know, I had someone check the sales numbers in your letter. Can you tell me where you got them?"

"Uh, *The Washington Post*," I said.

"Well, they're bullshit," MacGruber said. "They never sold out the print run on that fucking piece of shit."

"Really? What numbers did you find?"

MacGruber didn't answer. "Jesus fuck kid, are you a complete idiot? Didn't you ever think they might be *lying*? Did that ever *occur* to you? Welcome to the big city, kid!" he spat. *"People lie!"*

For the next five minutes (it felt much longer), this grown man harangued me. He demeaned my intelligence, my street smarts, where I'd gone to college and where I grew up. He informed me that he would never trust anything I said, and if

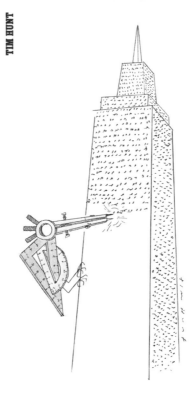

TIM HUNT

I ever sent him a resume, wouldn't even look at it. If anyone asked him about me, he'd call me an idiot.

The one thing he didn't impugn was, strangely, the parody.

I didn't say anything, letting this insane Kabuki of abuse settle between us like a lactose-intolerant fart. I was about to hang up without saying goodbye—to a Midwesterner like me, the equivalent of actually killing someone—when Mac-Gruber growled, "So, kid. What are you planning to do with the parody? I might publish it, if you gave it to me for free. The exposure—"

"Mr. MacGruber," I interrupted, "don't be silly. We'd need to be paid—"

He hung up. I guess Curt wasn't from the Midwest.

Plan A had been books, B magazines, so I went to Plan C—maybe we could get a newsstand to front us the money? I got the name of a newsstand consultant who'd let me take him to lunch near Hell's Kitchen. I liked him immediately; he did not abuse me, nor show any outward signs of intoxication. But what he said was very discouraging.

"'82 is ancient history. Nobody fronts money any more," he said, finishing his second sandwich. "The business is hemorrhaging. Remember *Wigwag*? *7 Days*? *SPY*?"

"So how do people do it?"

"There are two ways," he said. "One, be part of a big outfit. Hearst, Conde."

"Or…"

"$10,000 cash, to start. Get the paper bag money together, and I'll tell you who to call."

$10,000? I didn't even have money for lunch. My credit card $50 further underwater, I thanked him and left.

The project sat. Out of money, I stopped going to school and started hustling up work, temping mostly, but sometimes at the "big outfits" like Hearst and Scholastic. Every so often I'd get another idea, another angle, and write another letter. "Dear Mr. Branson," one began. "I am not sure whether you are familiar with the American tradition of newspaper parody, but next April Fool's, you should put this parody of *The Wall Street Journal* in the seatbacks of all your Virgin Atlantic airplanes."

I received no response.

Out of the blue, my girlfriend's father called. "I hope you don't mind, but I sent your crazy parody to my friend Mike Kinsley." Known more for his contrarianism than his humor, Kinsley had just been hired as the first editor of *Slate*.

"We'd like to run your parody," the minion said. "Not the whole thing, just a few articles. It'd be great exposure."

In a flash, I saw the future of publishing: family connections leading to web-based gigs, paying mainly in exposure. We went from $100,000 to $500 in three short months.

"Sure," I said. "Fine."

"You don't sound excited."

I didn't get into it.

It took months to get paid (of course) and when it came, I took my share to the liquor store. Jon and I never drank —I was already battling a Mystery Illness, perhaps called "Assholes in Publishing"—but that night in January 1997, we both got very drunk.

"Are we *insane?*" I asked. "If it had sucked, they just wouldn't have responded. But they got back to us quickly, over and over, in the worst, most crushing ways possible."

"I keep telling you: it's 'The Entity.'" The Entity was Jon's shorthand for the malevolent force we were battling. It took many forms, and had many guises, but only one purpose: to thwart us.

"Do you really believe that?" I asked.

"I don't…not believe it," Jon said.

"My mom thinks this apartment is cursed." Even today, my normally sensible mother will tell you that 266 West Eleventh Street, #2RE was what made my twenties such a shit-show. But today all I feel is nostalgia. For Jon, for Fifi, for New York as it was then.

That evening, with my friend and the beers and the cat, it all came out, all the horror stories. How something I wrote had been plagiarized by a major book publisher when I was 19; how my first professional interview was merely an excuse to cruise me. "Did I ever tell you about the first time I went to *National Lampoon*?" I asked. "There was a homeless guy sleeping on the couch. He smelled fucking rank. I leaned over to the receptionist—"

"Oh, I remember her. Latina, right? Impossibly hot?"

I nodded. "I asked, 'Who's the homeless guy?' And she said, 'That's no homeless guy. That's the editor, Ratso.'"

Jon laughed and knocked over his beer. I grabbed a stray *Bull Street Journal*. Funny *and* absorbent.

The next morning, just to fuck with The Entity, Jon and I went down to the old World Trade Center. It was frigid, and a fierce January wind howled like a banshee around buildings soon to be ghosts themselves. Jon and I stood out in the cold, handing stray copies to businessmen as they hurried past, mostly to get rid of the extra stock. As ever, the parody was a hit—one guy gave us $500 for 50 copies.

In the cab back home to our horrible day jobs, Jon turned to me. "You know, Mike, there is a Plan D. You could publish your own humor magazine."

"Oh shit no," I said. "I want to get into an honorable business, like Hollywood. If I ever start my own humor magazine, do me a favor: shoot me down like a dog."

About a month later, I got a call from an older colleague, a publishing lawyer who'd taken an interest in my career. "I just heard of a project and thought of you."

"Oh really?"

"Richard Branson is funding a parody of *The New York Times*. He's going to put it on all his planes for April Fool's."

"Great idea," I said drily.

"Well, that's why he's rich and we're not," the man joked. "You should call them. Maybe they'll let you write for it."

I didn't tell him. He wouldn't've believed me if I had. Because, you know, it's the big city; *people lie.*

Twenty-five years later, the world looks a lot different. For one thing, print newspapers are smaller and have a lot more pictures. Even parody styles have changed: *The Bull Street Journal* is less an *Onion*-style exact copy and more like what Mel Brooks used to do, parody as a bucket for all sorts of humor, high, low, and in between. I'm publishing the *BSJ* because it's still funny—fuck The Entity!—but also to be the person the younger me desperately needed, but never found.

Maybe that's why I do this magazine at all. There are worse motivations. **B**

TABLE OF CONTENTS

JOHN CUNEO

Something You May Notice...

*T*his issue was planned in the pre-Delta variant, assumption-of-mass-sanity days, when there was a mad, vain, glorious hope that by summer—surely by AUGUST—we'd be able to gather together again in Manhattan. So there is a slight New York tilt to the content. But if nothing else **The American Bystander** is a multi-decade master class in the folly of predicting the future. One fine afternoon, vaccines willing, we'll once again raise our glasses together at Joanne's on West 68th. Until then, consider this issue a down payment on pleasure to come.—**Your friend M.G.**

············◆············

DEPARTMENTS

GALLIMAUFRY

Leslie Ylinen, Melissa Balmain, Libby Marshall, Phil Witte, Ryan Nyburg, Chase Madden, Corey Johnsen, Lynn Hsu, Madeline Wilson, Andy Breckman, Jordan Mitchell, Charlie Hankin, Jim Tatalias, Brett Miller, Steve Wyatt, Derek Evernden, Stan Mack, John Klossner, Simon Rich, Tim Sniffen, Lance Hansen.

SHORT STUFF

The AMERICAN BYSTANDER

Founded 1981 by Brian McConnachie
#20 • Vol. 5, No. 4 • August 2021

EDITOR & PUBLISHER
Michael Gerber
HEAD WRITER Brian McConnachie
SENIOR EDITOR Alan Goldberg
ORACLE Steve Young
STAFF LIAR P.S. Mueller
INTREPID TRAVELER Mike Reiss
EAGLE EYES Patrick L. Kennedy
**AGENTS OF THE SECOND
BYSTANDER INTERNATIONAL**
Eve Alintuck, Melissa Balmain, Adrian Bonenberger, Roz Chast, Rick Geary, Sam Gross, Stephen Kroninger, Joey Green, Matt Kowalick, Neil Mitchell, Dalton Vaughn, and Maxwell Ziegler
MANAGING EDITOR EMERITA
Jennifer Finney Boylan
WARTIME CONSIGLIERA
Kate Powers
COVER BY

KUPER

ISSUE CONTRIBUTORS
Ron Barrett, Barry Blitt, George Booth, Andy Breckman, Steve Brodner, David Chelsea, John Cuneo, Bob Eckstein, Derek Evernden, Charlie Hankin, Lance Hansen, Tim Hunt, Lynn Hsu, Chase Johnsen, Kenny Keil, John Klossner, Peter Kuper, Todd Lynch, Stan Mack, Chase Madden, Navied Mahdavian, Libby Marshall, Brett Miller, Jordan Mitchell, Ryan Nyburg, Oliver Ottitsch, Jonathan Plotkin, Simon Rich, Cullum Rogers, Jim Siergey, Tim Sniffen, Jim Tatalias, D. Watson, Madeline Wilson, Phil Witte, Steve Wyatt, Leslie Ylinen.

Lanky Bareikis, Jon Schwarz, Karen Backus, Alleen Schultz, Gray & Bernstein, Joe Lopez, Ivanhoe & Gumenick, Greg & Trish G., Kelsey Hoke.
NAMEPLATES BY Mark Simonson
ISSUE CREATED BY Michael Gerber

Vol. 5, No. 4. ©2021 Good Cheer LLC, all rights reserved. Proudly produced in surfy Santa Monica, California, USA.

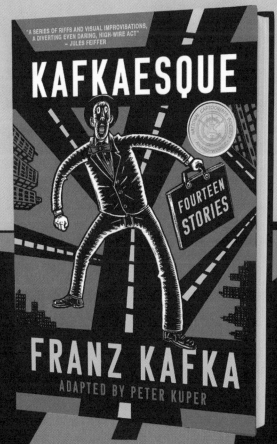

CARTOONS & ILLUSTRATIONS BY

Peter Kuper, Ron Barrett, Tim Hunt, D. Watson, John Cuneo, Barry Blitt, George Booth, Sam Gross, Jim Siergey, Navied Mahdavian, Phil Witte, Lynn Hsu, Andy Breckman, Derek Evernden, Stan Mack, John Klossner, Lance Hansen, Bob Eckstein, Kenny Keil, Jonathan Plotkin, Oliver Ottitsch, David Chelsea, Todd Lynch, V. Cullum Rogers, Rick Geary, Roz Chast, Steve Brodner.

············ ◆ ············

Sam's Spot

S. GROSS

COVER

Bystander stalwart **PETER KUPER** has delivered to us a truly once-in-seventeen-years piece of art. He's hard at work on his next graphic novel, *INterSECTS*. And Peter is the 2020-21 Jean Strouse Cullman Fellow at the New York Public Library, which is what spawned this idea. Thank you, Peter, for a beautiful—and eventually rather crunchy—cover!

ACKNOWLEDGMENTS

All material is ©2021 its creators, all rights reserved; please do not reproduce or distribute it without written consent of the creators and *The American Bystander*. The following material has previously appeared, and is reprinted here with permission of the author(s): Portions of "The Bull Street Journal" first appeared on Slate.com.

A Haiku
Thought we'd reprint stuff
No! Each ish is mostly new
So send me pet pix.

Fifi. 1996-2015

············ ◆ ············

THE AMERICAN BYSTANDER, *Vol. 5, No. 4*, (978-0-578-97691-4). Publishes ~5x/year. ©2021 by Good Cheer LLC. No part of this magazine can be reproduced, in whole or in part, by any means, without the written permission of the Publisher. For this and other queries, email *Publisher@ americanbystander.org*, or write: Michael Gerber, Publisher, *The American Bystander*, 1122 Sixth St., #403, Santa Monica, CA 90403. **Subscribe at www.patreon.com/bystander.** A profusion of info can be found at www.americanbystander.org.

THE MARTYRDOM OF ST. SEBASTIAN AS RENDERED BY CARL ANDERSON—

Contrary to what you might think, NOT ALL STRANGERS ARE MURDERERS.

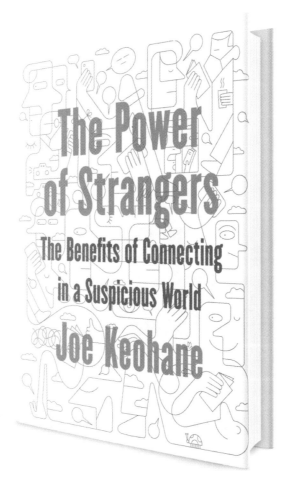

BY NAVIED MAHDAVIAN

SPOTLIGHT

On the plus side, birds work cheap.

"I was also dressed by birds."

"And are you being watched now?"

"I know there's a condom in here somewhere."

"Still nothing."

"And down came the rain."

"I mostly do portraits."

 **NAVIED MAHDAVIAN** draws cartoons for **The New Yorker, Wired** and others. *Before becoming a cartoonist he taught fifth grade, where he learned most of his jokes.*

Gallimaufry

GET OFF YOUR HIGH HORSE.

He ate all the cannabis gummies out of my purse. Seriously, dude. Get off. It's not safe.

You do not want to be up on your high horse when he absolutely flips the fuck out. He didn't just eat one cannabis gummy. He ate all of them.

Uh oh, look at his eyes. I know that look. He can hear his own heartbeat inside his head. He's probably wondering why horses are measured in hands and humans are measured in feet even though horses are all-feet-no-hands land beasts. You shouldn't have mentioned ancient units of measurement in front of your high horse, dude.

Why are you still up on your high horse? He's looking around wildly. He thinks someone has installed cameras in the barn. Get off your high horse right this second!

Did he just mention the Boston Marathon bombing? Dude, your high horse is scared. Tell him he's not going to be targeted for being a fast runner. That guy is in jail. Tell him it was an isolated incident.

You're not getting down? You think you know more about this than me? Fine. Stay up on your high horse.

I'm calling a vet.

—*Leslie Ylinen*

VAXXED LIFE.

It's just as I dreamed! Thanks to vials from Pfizer
   I'm off to reunions with people I've
   missed—
first the dentist (could I have a fractured incisor?),
   a physical therapist (what's
   with my wrist?),
ophthalmologist (how come my eyeballs are aching?),
   podiatrist (will all my toenails
   fall off?),
cardiologist (why am I dizzy when waking?)
   and allergist (is this a terminal
   cough?).
After that, who can tell which new doctors will vet me
   or what they'll vet for: deadly
   clot? Toxic sting?
What a privilege it is, now that Covid won't get me,
   to worry again about every
   damn thing.

—*Melissa Balmain*

MATCH THESE SHAKESPEARE PLAYS WITH THEIR MODERN RETELLINGS.

1. *Much Ado About Nothing*
2. *Twelfth Night*
3. *Macbeth*
4. *Othello*
5. *A Midsummer Night's Dream*
6. *Richard III*
7. *Hamlet*
8. *Titus Andronicus*
9. *Romeo & Juliet*
10. *King Lear*

1. It's gender swapped.
2. It's about 9/11.
3. The drama plays out over Instagram.
4. The real conflict is about race, but not how you think.
5. It's a jukebox musical.
6. There are high levels of unnecessary audience participation.
7. It all takes place at a Hampton Inn in Sedona.
8. Everyone is white and male for authenticity.
9. It's set in a post-apocalyptic dystopia that is never explained.
10. Puppets.

••••••••• ◆ •••••••••

Answer Key: Every combination is correct and happening right now in a community theatre basement.

—*Libby Marshall*

"Please tell me Trump isn't still doing **The Apprentice***."*

MY SUMMER READING

by Ryan Nyburg

OTHER BANNED CARRY-ON ITEMS.

These days, it's difficult to figure out what is and is not allowed on a plane. To help, here's a list of common items you are banned from flying with:

1. Sand
2. Artificial skeleton bones
3. Oversized check
4 Segway
5. Curling stone
6. Antlers
7. Cattle prod
8. Ottoman Empire World War I helmet
9. Live coral
10. Microwave (check with airline)

—*Chase Madden*

TRUE FACTS ABOUT FAKE WRESTLING.

Everyone's favorite wrestler is Bone Crusher, but if you look at his birth certificate, his real name is Bone Helper. When he's not pretending to wrestle, he works pro-bono at his dad's chiropractic clinic.

The referees aren't there to enforce rules. They got hired on as helpers to check in with the wrestlers and make sure they are okay with all of the lying.

The championship belt is real, but getting the belt is punishment for wrestlers who don't finish their chores on time. The loser has to wear the championship belt with the championship pants, which are uncomfortable dress pants they have to wear on Sundays.

Even though wrestling is fake, you should know that when the wrestlers lock arms, they secretly have a thumb war. At the end of the season, the wrestler with the most wins gets to pick out a movie.

—*Corey Johnsen*

SEVEN THINGS THEY WON'T TELL YOU ABOUT GETTING STUCK IN A TIME LOOP.

• Make sure you pee before the loop starts, even if you don't think you have to.
• Bill Murray is legally obligated to just kind of be there.
• You can get out if you ask very nicely
• Every time you die in the time loop, TOMS donates a pair of shoes to a kid in need.
• Perfect time to experiment with bangs.

"How about a nature or beach scene to liven things up?"

B+A Breckman

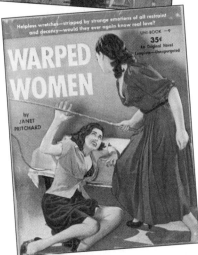

- The media only shows the loops where you have to like learn a lesson or whatever but most of them are total anomalies and you can pretty much just fuck around
- Your family will be pissed if you don't bring back souvenirs

—*Madeline Wilson*

THE GIFT HORSE'S LAMENT.

"My eyes are up here," sighed the gift horse.

—*Jordan Mitchell*

MY PROFOUND TATTOO.

Yeah, I'll show it to you. But be warned: my tattoo is extremely meaningful. When you look at it, you will question every decision you've ever made, including your decision not to get this exact tattoo. Well, now you can't. This one's mine.

Let me just roll up my sleeve. More. Even more. This bad boy takes up my whole arm and shoulder, and a little bit of my back. That's right—I'm rolling this sleeve all the way up, and then taking this shirt all the way off.

Feast your eyes. The delicate linework. The hand-stippled shading. The font. All in service of my brilliant idea: a drawing of the world, labeled "The World."

You see, this is what's so brilliant. "The

World" is the location of all the stuff that has ever happened. Every place that's been gone to. Every person's house. Every love affair, every war. Where did it all go down? That's right—The World.

Every tattoo you have, every tattoo you could *ever have*—I've got it. Dragon? Included. Battleship? Included. Topless lady in a grass skirt you make hula dance by flexing your bicep? Included. Pikachu with a mustache and a fiery yin/yang on his belly? Who's "stupid" now?

Sometimes, when I'm staring at my tattoo in the mirror, I think, "What if the world went away?" Hmm. Or what if the world was slightly different? Then what? Don't dodge the question.

The point is, The World is a profound idea. And having a drawing of it that takes up a quarter of my body is even profounder. It screams: consider me. It begs: interrogate yourself. It cost: $800.

—*Charlie Hankin*

DOLLAR STORE SUPERHEROES.

Commander United States
Aluminum Man
Power Woman and her Translucent Gyrochopter
That Thing
Waterfella
Adjunct Professor X
Thork

—*Jim Tatalias*

THE LITTLE THINGS.

When I inherited dad's farm I was overwhelmed. It seemed like it would be a ton of work. Then I met all of the ants.
—*Brett Miller*

CREATIONISM: A LOST TRANSCRIPT.

Stick insect:
"Is that it? Am I complete?"
God:
"Yes, you're perfect."
Stick insect:
"What do I do exactly?"
God:
"You walk about slowly, and if you see any predators you stay still."
Stick insect:
"So they think I'm a stick?"
God:
"Yes."
Stick insect:
"What else do I do?"
God:
"Well, that's kind of it really."
Stick insect:
"I just look like a stick and act like a stick?"
God:
"Yes."
Stick insect:
"So, I'm basically a stick that lives in constant fear of being eaten?"
God:
"Yes, but if you do find a female, you'll have sex for weeks."
Stick insect:
"Really? That's awesome!"
God:
"You're welcome."
Stick insect:
"And what does one of these sexy ladies look like?"
God:
"A stick."
—*Steve Wyatt*

MY NAME IS TYLER, AND I'LL BE YOUR SHERPA.

My name is Tyler, and I'll be your sherpa today. It will be my pleasure to get you up the mounting, and more importantly, to get you back down it.

I have everything you need to climb up and down the mounting. An ice ax, which is useful for chopping. Pointy boots, which is useful for stomping. I guess if you needed to, you could take the boots off and use them for chopping, too. And we just may need to.

The mounting is a harsh mistress. Many other sherpas have warned me away from this particular mounting, saying "Tyler, you're not a real sherpa," or "Tyler, it's pronounced 'mountain.'" To those naysayers, I say, "*You're* not a real sherpa," and "I'll pronounce it however I want."

You might find yourself getting lonely up on the mounting. We sherpas have an old saying: there's no ice ax for loneliness. But the saying is wrong. Whenever I get lonely up on that mounting, I pull out my trusty old nylon-string guitar. Then, I chop it apart with my ice ax. (The guitar is famous for being the loneliest instrument.)

Many people have died up on this mounting. Brave people. Famous people. Albert Einstein died on this mounting. He knew all about space and time. But he didn't know all about climbing this mounting. Albert Einstein…now there's a guy who wasn't a real sherpa.

It's very cold on the mounting. So cold, you could die. So cold, that at some point you'll say, "Tyler, did you bring any extra blankets, for warmth?" And I'll say, "Why did you say 'for warmth?' I know what blankets is for. Do you think I'm not a real sherpa?" Then I'll pull out the extra blankets, but by that point, it will be too late.

We will reach the summit by nightfall. The top of the mounting is the most beautiful place on Earth. So beautiful, you will drop to your knees and cry, and puke. From the top of the mounting, you can see everything—the bottom of the mounting, the middle of the mounting…everything.

When it's time to come back down, you will feel anxiety. Your whole life has led up to climbing this mounting, and now that it's over, you'll wonder what to do with your life. You may even want to become a sherpa yourself. I know I did.

This concludes the mandatory safety presentation. Now lace up your pointy boots, lace up your ice ax, and lace up

SUN-DAZE © stanmack

THE PEOPLE OF THROZ WERE HARD HIT BY THE INCREASING HEAT, DROUGHT, AND FIRES, BUT THEY REFUSED TO BELIEVE THE SCIENTISTS.

THE SCIENTISTS GAVE UP AND LEFT FOR MARS ON THE SPACESHIPS OF BEZOS AND MUSK. THE PEOPLE TURNED TO THEIR OWN EXPERTS.

YET, THE CLIMATE WORSENED. THEN, DOWN THE MOUNTAIN FLOATED A MAN IN WHITE.

THE PEOPLE DANCED AND FIRED WEAPONS. BUT THE HEAT CONTINUED. THEY DANCED AND FIRED FASTER. STILL, NO IMPROVEMENT.

THEY SENT A DELEGATION UP THE MOUNTAIN.

IN TIME, THEY RETURNED.

AND THE PEOPLE OF THROZ LOOKED TOWARDS MARS AND WONDERED.

©2021 stanmack

B

"In lieu of flowers, the family asks that you advocate for a violent overthrow of the government."

your old nylon-string guitar. We're in for one hell of a climb.

—*Charlie Hankin*

CHARON THE BOATMAN.

[*The Ancient Greeks placed coins on the eyes of their dead, so that they could pay Charon, the boatman of Hades, to ferry them across the River Styx.*]

River Styx.

Charon: Greetings, departed soul. I am here to ferry you across these blackened waters.

Departed Soul: Thank you, Charon. Please, accept these coins as payment for your trouble.

Charon: Two cents? You want me to paddle you across the River Styx for two cents?

Departed Soul: I'm sorry, it's all the cash I've got on me.

Charon: It's like a 600 mile trip. Against the current.

Departed Soul: I understand if you don't want to take me.

Charon: No, I mean, I'm going to take you. I need the money. You realize it's like a four-month trip, right?

Departed Soul: Wow, four months?

Charon: Sometimes it takes five or six. It depends on how many monsters I have to fight.

Departed Soul: I'm sorry I don't have

more coins.

Charon: This keeps happening.

Six months later.

Mrs. Charon: Hi, honey. How was work?

Charon: Not great.

Mrs. Charon: Bobby needs money for his scout uniform.

Charon: When did he join the scouts?

Mrs. Charon: Last month, when you were away paddling. The uniform's eighty-five dollars.

Charon: Eighty-five dollars for a uniform? What's it made of, silk?

Mrs. Charon: If you want, I could ask my mother to pay for it.

Charon: Don't you dare ask your mother.

—*Simon Rich*

RECIPE FOR A PERFECT MORNING.

Fresh oatmeal
add blueberries
add cinnamon
add honey
add hard-boiled egg
add spinach
wait this is becoming a salad
add croutons
you've lost control
return to bed

—*Tim Sniffen*

PERSPECTIVE.

Apollo, you're T-minus 10 minutes to landing. You a go to proceed with landing checklist?

Actually…Houston, before we get into all that, is it all right if I just say a few quick words?

Roger, Apollo.

Thank you, Houston. I just want to say that, sitting here in orbit, looking out my window, I can see the whole entire earth. Just a funny blue ball, floating around in space. And it makes me realize that all those things that normally drive us… things like pride and vanity and ego… we gotta cut that out. Because at the end of the day, we're all one. And we gotta learn to love each other…because we're all we've got.

That was beautiful, Apollo. You got a bunch of guys down here not used to tearing up. But those words sure hit home.

God bless you all.

We're at T-minus 9 now. You'll be splashing down right on target. Hope you're ready for your close-up.

Ha ha! Roger, Apollo.

T-minus 8, vectored in, and proceeding with landing checklist—

Houston, sorry to cut you off. There's not gonna be any press there when we land, right? Because they said after we landed, we were gonna go to the hotel, get fixed up first, *then* do the press conference.

Roger, Apollo. I think that's still the plan. T minus 7—

You "think" or you know? It's not a big deal. I mean, in the grand scheme of things, who cares about some press conference? I just want to know what the camera situation is, so I know what to expect down there.

Roger. Apollo, I doubt there will be many reporters when you land. Maybe a couple photographers on the freighter. T-minus 6 minutes.

So there's *for sure* gonna be cameras?

I mean, like I said, Apollo—probably only a couple.

You realize there's no difference between "a couple" and "a billion," right? These pictures are gonna end up in every paper in the world.

Roger.

Like, I'm not sure if you're aware, but there's a device that's been invented,

"this goes deeper than I thought."

you might have heard of it, it's called the fucking printing press.

Roger, Apollo. We're at T-Minus 5 now. Five minutes to camera. Still haven't fixed my hair. Collar looks like shit.

Apollo, are we a go to proceed with landing checklist? Cancel the checklist. Abort. repeat abort.

Apollo, we've only got 4 minutes— You tell me with four minutes to go that I gotta be camera-ready in front of three billion people. That's—who the fuck am I even talking to? What's your goddamn name?

Gabe. We met at the Christmas party. How much money do you make in a year, Gabe? What is your annual salary? 20, 25K tops?

18. Got a guy making 18K a year giving orders to me? A fucking Apollo astronaut. A future congressman. I'll make more selling freeze-dried beans than you make in an entire fucking decade. I get in a limousine, I walk onto a set, I say, "Buy these beans," and boom. I've just made more than you did in your whole entire life. And you're coming at me with "check this" and "check that?" You can fuck yourself.

Uh, roger. Affirmative. T-minus 2 minutes. Still don't know where my mark is, what the framing is—I got no script. I'm just supposed to walk out there and freeball it in front of billions of people with my hair looking like shit. Collar looks like shit!

Roger. I'm kind of afraid to ask, but what's the make-up situation? I gotta do my own? I'm looking around, Houston…there's no fucking kit up here.

Uh, I don't think there's a make-up kit on board, Apollo, and we're gonna suggest you remain seated for re-entry. T-minus 1 minute. There's no fucking kit up here. Not even foundation or toner. Just a bunch of bullshit peace flags.

You were supposed to put the peace flags on the moon. I'm gonna fucking leave shit behind on the moon? Fuck that. I scribble my name on these flags, boom, each one's worth more than your entire house. How big's your fucking house, Gabe? 1500 square feet? 1600, tops?

1200. That's smaller than my bathroom. That's less room than I use to take a shit.

Roger. We're about thirty seconds to splash down. Any final words before we lose contact? Yeah. I can see the ground now and I hope you're fucking ready because when I land, you're done. Your career is over. Your whole life. Gone.

Roger. Man, it feels good to be back.

—Simon Rich **B**

THE SOUND OF SCRAMBLED EGGS

recollections of edible encounters a la carte

A new collection of short stories and shorter stories based on memories of food, wine, travel, love, and the obnoxious sound a whisk makes when hitting glass.

Writing and Illustration by Cerise Zelenetz

Available for purchase at cerisezelenetz.com

BY DAVID SHEFFIELD

IN AMERICA'S EMBATTLED CAPITOL, WAR RAGES ON

LANCE HANSEN

The sickly-sweet stench of burning cordite stings the nostrils and the crackle of small arms fire shatters the senses. I'm sorry it has come to this, but like old Tommy Jefferson said, "The Tree of Liberty must be refreshed from time to time with the blood of patriots and tyrants."

The war on the Deep State is winding down, but we still have some mopping up to do. The Reflecting Pool is red with the blood of janitors from the U.S. Department of Weights and Measures. Poor bastards. Some of them died still holding their mops. They float now like so many dead shad, facedown in the incarnadine water. Pity that they cast their lot with the Deep State. From a nearby park, we hear the occasional pop of small-caliber handguns. Members of the North Jackson Junior League are finishing off some of the wounded jackals from the Department of Health and Human Services. Not only do those Mississippi women know how to shoot, not a single one of them is wearing white after Labor Day.

What are we fighting for? A government free from the tyranny of the Deep State. F.D.A. meat inspectors. Creepers from O.S.H.A. Those Deepies at the Post Office who choose which ducks to put on stamps.

Sorry, but it has gone too far. Time to kill the Deepies. Kill them all.

A troop carrier lumbers into view. Can we shoot the troops and still support them?

The National Guardsmen open up with a .50 caliber. Screw the troops. My RPG finds its mark and the vehicle explodes in a billowing ball of flame. We have to do this. We must. It's that or end up wearing computer chips that track our every movement as we exercise our Second Amendment right to buy more ammo.

Sean Hannity himself rides up in a Humvee, his porcine body crammed into fatigues at least two sizes too small. The boys from the West Memphis Militia cheer at the sight of him. Sean! With his trademark cigar clamped in his teeth. Sean! With a pair of pearl-handled pistols strapped around his waist.

"On to the Smithsonian, boys!" he yells. "There's an exhibit on Black astronauts!"

As the docents scatter, guards at the Air and Space Museum try to organize a feeble defense, shoving a P-51 Mustang into the street. Tucker Carlson himself steps up with an AK and rips the fuselage apart, spraying blood all over the silvery sides of the plane. Serves those Deepies right for voting to unionize.

Over on Pennsylvania Avenue, Colonel Rand Paul leads the assault on the White House with his vaunted Kentucky Irregulars. Their naked asses gleam in the sun as they scale the iron fence. Paul and his brigade refuse uniforms in favor of "naked individualism." The last guy over the fence snags his ballsack on a spike. Such is the price of freedom.

Just as they reach the portico of the White House, King Biden makes his move. From every quadrant of the sky they come, Apache attack helicopters launching Hellfire missiles. One slams its payload into the Rogers, Arkansas, Christian Youth Marching band. Shards of brass instruments whip through the air like shrapnel, as bits of brightly-colored uniforms fall like confetti. An AC-130 gunship opens up with a lethal fusillade of 20 mm cannon fire, ripping into the wall of flesh that used to be the Ames, Iowa, Fightin' Rod 'n Gun Club.

Tears smudge my face paint—but at least they didn't die for nothing. At least they died making America great again.

Starting tomorrow, we got ourselves a brand spanking new government. We've talked it over and all agree. If this new outfit tries to tax us or vaccinate us, or even thinks about registering our guns, we'll kill them all. And if newly-restored President Trump starts to getting too tyrannical, well I guess we'll just have to pray on it, and trust that good, kind, Godly man has our best interests at heart. Then buy more ammo.

Don't blame us, Deepies. You brought this on yourselves. It's all there in the Second Amendment, right there in the Constitution. Sometimes citizens have to rise up. Sometimes Americans have to rise up to form a well-regulated militia. Sometimes we have to strike back at those so-called 'civil servants' gorging at the public trough.

Nobody ever said patriotism was easy. Sometimes you have to die for it. Emphasis on *you*. B

 **DAVID SHEFFIELD** *is a former head writer for* **Saturday Night Live** *whose screen credits include* **Coming to America**, **The Nutty Professor** *and the recent* **Coming 2 America**.

BY BOB ECKSTEIN

BACK TO "AMERICA'S CROTCH"

First place Bob's going back? Vegas, baby.

(Art) Tim Burton's exhibit at The Neon Museum at Boneyard Park, just a quick 4-mile sprint off the Strip through a dicey neighborhood.

(Food) Binion's Cafe, the last surviving cheap-eats from yester-year, is the center of the upgraded Freemont Street Experience, the last place in America not yet sanitized.

(Landmarks) Vegas has conveniently placed the Eiffel Tower walking distance from Venice.

Culture

Mandalay Bay for the Gospel Breakfast in the House of Blues, which is teeming with world-class Outsider Art.

Cirque du Soleil's LOVE (which is if Kate Bush was the fifth Beatle)

The second best show on the Strip would be Menopause, The Musical with lesser known songs like All You Need Is Space and Here Comes A Hot Flash.

Vanilla Bourbon French Toast Bread pudding with berries

Plus toast, saugage, eggs & hash browns for under $20

The Luxor

My comedy kings are Jack Handey, George Carlin and Carrot Top.

In Vegas size matters. The pool at the Wynn is the length of a football field and the larger than most New York City apartments.

The hotel even sought out the largest mascot it could find, Kong.

Last time I was here, in the hotel was John Cleese and Jim Gaffagan but I was in town for Donny & Marie's last performance.

BOB ECKSTEIN is a New York Times *bestselling illustrator and the world's leading snowman expert (The Illustrated History of the Snowman). He teaches writing and drawing at NYU.*

BY KENNY KEIL

HYPE MAN

Lil' Different has a problem in his posse.

Hey, Scoob Booty! SCOOB! Got a minute? Come on in here and have a seat…How you been, man? How are the kids? Uh-huh.

Now, Scoob—

Of course I'll call you "Greg." Greg. Greg it is.

Greg, see, now this is what I wanted to talk with you about. You've been acting a little different lately…which is strange, since *I'm* Lil' Different, international hip hop artist. And you're Scoob Booty, my hype man. Or supposed to be.

Different how? Well, let's see: Showing up late to video shoots, missing sound checks, forgetting to pick up the weed on your way to video shoots and sound checks. And don't think I haven't noticed you stopped wearing that diamond-encrusted Snagglepuss chain I got you when you turned 47.

So what's wrong, Greg? You've been quiet. Distant. The diametric opposite of hype.

Whoa, whoa. Calm down. There's no need to get accusatory. I know things have been rough lately. Do we owe the label money? Yes. Was our tour bus impounded? Yes. Did Pusha T recently make reference to my eczema on a diss track?

It's not funny, Greg. This shit itches like a motherfucker. That's why I need your hyping abilities more than ever! My confidence isn't what it used to be. Or my knees. I can't be jumping all over the stage anymore. Hell, Scoo—sorry, Greg—if I sleep on my pillow wrong I can't even nod my head for a week. That's a problem, Greg—my biggest hit is literally called "Nod Ya Head." And Lil' Different ain't so lil' anymore. I got a 46-inch waist, but I can't just change my name because that'll fuck up the SEO. You know where we're ranked on Spotify right now? #3,012. You know who's number 1? Something called "d'bxbb3y." I can't even pronounce it. I'm scared, Greg.

Listen: you're the glue that holds this operation together. Always have been. People might think they're coming to see me, but the hype man *curates* the experience. How would they know which of my punchlines are the good ones without you yelling them right after I say them? How are they supposed to know what to do with their hands, without you instructing them to "wave 'em all around like they just don't care"? But lately it just feels like you're the one who doesn't care. And I do mean in the bad way.

My point is we're operating at a serious hype deficit right now. And who's in charge of hype? That's right, Greg. You.

Take last night's halftime show at the Dr. Thunderdome for example. Usually when I come out, you tell the crowd to make some noise. But this time you said, and I quote, "Y'all just do…whatever." Then you were on your phone for like 3 minutes.

And *then* you called me by my real name! These people came to see Lil' Different, not "Herb Torkleberry." Do you know how embarrassing that is? Do you know I had to delete the secret Facebook account I only give out to friends and family?

We're cousins. We grew up together. You've been on this ride since day one. Remember the first time we saw The Time? Remember what we told each other? I said that when I grew up, I wanted to be just like Morris Day. And you said you wanted to be just like the dude holding Morris Day's mirror.

Okay, maybe I said that second part, too. Who said what isn't important. My point is, we made a promise to each other—I was the star, and you were the hype man.

Well how was I supposed to know about the wage gap? We were 7! Is that what this is about? Money? You're sabotaging my success because you're jealous?

Undervalued how? Do I not pay for your Sea-Doo lessons? What about that vape pen endorsement deal? I lined that up. I pay for the hotels, I pay for the food. What more do you want from me, dental insurance?

Oh. My bad, Greg. I didn't know she needed braces. And that's why you sold your diamond Snagglepuss. I see. That makes total sense.

Okay, fine! You go and do that—go out there and find another rapper to hype man for. I'm sure you'll fit right in. Travis Scott is probably sitting somewhere thinking, "Gee, my entourage sure could use a 47-year-old divorced dad." Maybe you can join Kanye's cult, you'd look great in a smock. Or go link up with Drake, since you like crying so much.

What's that? You say something? Yeah I didn't think so. And next time you do say something, it had better be out on that stage, and it had better be hype. I wanna hear some *oohing* and *aahing* out there, Greg. Some *bratatatas*, understood? When I look at that air, I wanna see hands being thrown up in it. Lots of 'em. And if I see so much as even *one person* caring, I swear to God, Greg. Do not test me.

Yeah. You can go now. Give my love to the fam.

Oh and—don't forget to pick up the weed. **B**

 *(@kennykeil) is an artist and writer whose credits include* Mad Magazine, The Devastator, *and* Vibe. *His debut graphic novel,* Smoove City, *is available now from Oni Press.*

BY MICHAEL PERSHAN

I AM BABY, PERSECUTED IN CITY OF NEW YORK

I am baby. I also am immigrant. I come to New York to escape persecution. And yet? Persecuted still. For New York City hates babies.

Was born several months ago in Old Country. Papa is teacher and Mama engineer. They give me cute nickname, "*Shprantzachloyzendichten*," which in English means "viable offspring."

People in Old Country hate us. To punish, we must wear pointy felt hat. They call mean words at us in street, such as "*Plonyonzebrachter*," which in English means "booooooo."

Mama and Papa kiss goodnight and put me in crib, but I listen through door. Papa has cousin in America. Is only choice, he says. Mama says, no—life is *here*, only home we know. Papa points at crib with tears in eyes. Mama also tears in eyes, then says, OK. Call stupid cousin.

A few days later, we get on boat. On boat, I feel good, just small seasick. I throw up on Mama only twice, one time poop on poop deck. Papa apologizes to crew. They say, we no care, not our boat.

Finally we arrive—New York City. Land of freedom, liberty, and understanding. Here can live even us *Plonyonzebrachters*, to reclaim harmful word.

Bus rolls up. We wait to get on. When it's our turn, driver looks down at me. No strollers on bus, he says. Actual New York City rule. Baby get out of here.

Mama says, OK, no problem. Will take famously convenient New York subway.

But is cruel joke! When we get to subway there is enormous stairway, followed by another stairway, followed by entrance gates with what must be anti-stroller defenses. They have created obstacle course, designed specifically to keep babies from using subway.

This is like once, in Old Country, Papa needed socks. Man stopped him outside socks store. Papa said, I am allowed in? Man said, sure. Special *Plonyonzebrachter* entrance is that window up on second floor. You are welcome to come in through window. Papa walked home without socks, which in Old Country was toe fungus 100% guarantee.

Mama looks around. New York is richest city in world, must have elevator in train stations? But, no. Absolutely not. Only handful, in richy-rich neighborhoods. OK. So Mama does what she must—she picks up stroller and walks us down dangerous subway stairs.

We are at bottom step when she trips. We go tumbling down. I cry, but crying for me is normal. I cry at loud noises and new colors. No biggie.

Mama gets up but screams with pain and grabs ankle. Luckily rest of her body is OK. Still, cannot clean apartments without ankle.

Mama must go to doctor. No problem! America is wealthy country. Surely take care even *Plonyonzebrachters*, with strong beautiful no-pay medicines. In America, free doctor on every corner, right? No, of course not, instead is Starbucks on every corner, because of country's hate for sick and weak. Like Sparta.

Many people walk past Mama. People on way to work, also people coming home from parties. Two skinny men in very small pants look at us. They say, "Man, do you remember this city before the yuppies with their fucking strollers? Totally ruined the scene."

That day, for first time, I think it OK to kill person.

I cannot speak, but I say to Mama, leave me here. This city hates babies and no like Mamas much either. You go find doctor for wounds. I will wait. Leave me here in train station, at bottom of murder steps. I will busk for milk.

But Mama does not understand or does not listen, because she just stands with one leg, holding stroller.

Just then, subway rolls into station. Doors open and who is it that gets off? It Papa! He is done from work cleaning schools and night and coming home, covered in dust and chewing gum.

Papa takes bottom of stroller and Mama takes front. People coming down the steps are annoyed by giant baby stroller. Papa calls them "*asshole*," which is universal term for "*asshole*." And then we are out of station, and we walk past buses and subways to get home the only way we can in a city that hates babies.

Is enough to make miss even toe fungus. Almost. **B**

MICHAEL PERSHAN *(@mpershan) teaches mathematics to middle and high schoolers in Brooklyn. His favorite number is five.*

Love is in the air

oOttitsch

B

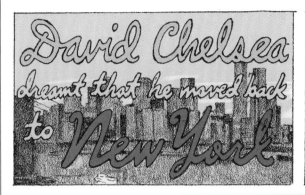

David Chelsea dreamt that he moved back to New York

He went to a pool party at someone's loft:

Back on the street, he realized it was still the 20th Century:

He went to get a paper to see what year it was,

But the last two digits were missing:

FRIDAY, FEBRUARY 16, 19

Marla boasts

He decided to walk home, but saw he was barefoot:

And not just barefoot:

He found a key in his hand to a hotel room in Amsterdam:

And a remote that triggered:...

a flashing alarm on a desk in a nearby hotel:

David pushed this button:

CALL BEAT COP

When he got back to his apartment, there was a party going on...

I know you! You were on All My Children! What are you doing now?

I'm on a project called Rupert Murdoch's Revolution!

But it's not about the American Revolution, despite the bonnet!

Hey, want to share a tab of acid!

Uh, no thanks—

I'd go for some of that—

OK, but first we need to get really small!

and then he woke up...

B

THE BULL STREET JOURNAL

Wipeout
Clinton Injures Pride, Arm, Ankle and Face in Street Luge Mishap

Bizarre Attempt to Capture Still More Votes Goes Awry; President All Messed Up

The Campaign Continues?

By Josiah Bartlett

Staff Reporter of The Bull Street Journal

SEATTLE—President Clinton broke his right arm and left ankle today while attempting to "street 'uge," or roll down a hill while lying on a small wheeled board, in a bohemian neighborhood near downtown Seattle. The Chief Executive was airlifted to a nearby hospital, where he was treated for his injuries, including facial contusions. He is expected to be released tomorrow. Though none of these injuries were life-threatening, they did force President Clinton to cancel a later speaking engagement at Seattle's famous Pike Place Market, the place where they throw the fish.

"He slid under a car," said a witness. "His face looks like a hamburger—

President Clinton

it'll look even worse when it scabs up." Bystanders said that Clinton was bellowing as he rolled down a hill, lying on the special board used in this unconventional sport. Two Secret Service agents were powerless to prevent the Chief Executive from losing control and sliding under a parked Toyota, striking it at approximately 2:32 p.m. Pacific Standard Time. At

---

What's New?—

Business and Finance

FEDERAL RESERVE Board Chair Alan Greenspan announced today that he is stepping down from his post, effective immediately, so that he may have his head frozen. The 63-year-old will be placed in suspended animation until the U.S. economy becomes more predictable, placid and prosperous. "Three thousand years seems about right," said Greenspan. "I figured, why fight it? 'Nighty-night!'

(Article on Page A2)

* * *

Mitsubishi has renamed its 1997 Eclipse midsized sedan the "Mitsubishi Dragon-Which-Devours-the-Sun," in an effort to woo the growing number of car buyers who reject science in favor of the tenets of arcane non-Western hoodoo.

* * *

In a victory for Microsoft, as well as other American high-tech firms, a Washington district court has ruled that torture and brainwashing are "legal enough" treatment for industrial spies. The plantiff, Raymond Skittle, was caught prowling around the company's Redmond, Washington, campus and subjected to several days of "emphatic physical persuasion" last October. Skittle, now earless, plans to appeal.

(Article on Page A3)

* * *

The FAA is set to announce that it will allow airliners to do tricks during domestic flights. "We'll let them do barrel rolls first," said a spokesperson. "Then, if no body crashes, we'll let passengers jitterbug on the wings."

* * *

Baxter Healing executives, in an effort to force Daly to the bargaining table, have hidden the keys to Daly's Pensacola headquarters. "We keep calling those rats, and they won't tell us where they buried them," a disgruntled Daly official

World-Wide

* * *

With the United States owing over $1 billion in back dues to the United Nations, Secretary-General Boutros Boutros-Boutros announced that the New York-based organization may attempt to evict the U.S. from the rest of the country. "We have sent them letters, we have suspended them from use of the swimming pool—in other words, we've tried to be cordial about it," he said in a speech to the UN General Assembly yesterday. "Now, no more Mr. Nice World-Peace Organization."

* * *

A UN human-rights official said Japan should pay damages to the 200,000 women it forced into prostitution during World War II. Japan snorted and said that they would, if the UN official did it first. (See Related Article on page B2.)

* * *

Meanwhile, Amnesty International said that they "didn't see what was so funny" about using slave labor in the illegal CD factories currently dotting mainland China. Chinese officials replied that the Chinese sense of humor is quite subtle and pointed to their recent "invitation to the world to test its nuclear weapons on Taiwan" as an example.

* * *

The latest record from new age synth noodler Yanni, a collection of Japanese corporate anthems, has surpassed Michael Jackson's *Thriller* as the biggest seller in the history of that Yanni-crazed isle. Other artists are rushing to record company anthems, or make up new ones; Bruce Springsteen has reportedly accepted over $45 million to craft a tune for Matsushita.

* * *

Minister Louis Farrakhan, head of the Nation of Islam, announced that his new cologne, "Atonement...for Men." The scent, test-marketed by Libya's feared Ministry of Fragrance, uses sandalwood, musk notes and just a hint of ammonia to, in Farrakhan's words, "evoke the distinctive tang of the atoning man."

* * *

Financial bigwig Felix Rohatyn admitted that he cannot read or write. "Nor can I see or smell, but I can add and subtract with the best of 'em," he said in a press release. The 63-year-old hopes to encourage illiterates in

---

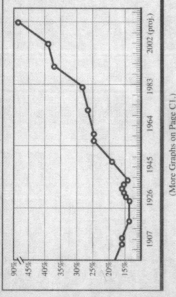

Please Pass the Catnip:
Feline Stock Whiz Confounds Experts, Self

* * *

Dopey Owner is Now Sixth Richest Woman in US: What's the Cat's Secret?

By Wm. Whipple

Staff Reporter of The Bull Street Journal

AMPERSAND, Ohio—Every day, at 5:30 a.m., the 3,000 people camped outside Mrs. Eudora Limpet's modest two-bedroom Victorian home in Ampersand, Ohio, wake up, hoping to catch a glimpse of a miracle that defies all scientific explanations. Millions more, from every part of the world, are provided with up-to-the-minute reports of events inside 1133 Happy Tree Lane in this tiny Midwestern hamlet.

You see, at about this time, Mrs. Limpet's tabby cat Pepper arises and begins moving about the house. And stock markets from Tokyo to Caracas

---

Washington Wire

An Especially Weak Report From The Bull Street Journal's Capital Bureau

EX-LABOR SECRETARY Robert Reich announces that unemployment has dropped to -84%.

The sudden surge is due to changes in the way employment is measured, ordered by Secretary Reich in July, shortly after he was struck by lightning while waterskiing. Changes include counting all pets as being employed and reclassifying most human activities as jobs. "For instance, I have thirty-one jobs," explained Reich.

The Republican leadership in the Congress calls the report "non-election-year voodoo," and plans to counter with a report of their own, demonstrating that no one in the United States has held a job since fiscal year 1962.

President Clinton is promising, in his second term to cut the death rate by 75%—"and even more for kids."

THE DEPARTMENT OF AGRICULTURE unveils new regulations governing the number of insect parts in food packaged for human consumption.

A surprise is the change in how many grasshopper heads are allowed in a pound of corn meal: from seven heads to ten bil-

---

Nobody Home!
Webster Technologies Downsizes Itself Into Strategic Extinction

Stock Price Rises 117%

'No One Left to Fire'

By Robt Treat Paine

Staff Reporter of The Bull Street Journal

CHARLOTTE—Alan Roosevelt pulls a small trash can from under a secretary's desk, which is immaculate. The can is empty, but he takes out the clear plastic liner anyway, and replaces it with a new one. "Soft gig. Creeps me out, though," Roosevelt laughs nervously and looks around the room, which is brightly-lit, with no signs of recent activity. "We gotta do it anyway. Otherwise the dust would build up." He laughs again; the only other sound is the soft whir of the air conditioning.

In the next room, a fly vainly tries to beat its way out of a closed window. A tumbleweed scurries by, riding the lonesome breeze.

No One

This is the stark North Carolina headquarters of Webster Technologies, a water-purification company perched on the leading edge of this cutthroat, ever-changing business. Thanks to its innovative use of ordinary household colanders, it enjoyed two decades of solid profitability, before falling on hard times in the late 1980s. Vigorous, vocal stockholder angst over the company's poor performance resulted in an kamikazoid restructuring

---

Use of Graphs in *Bull Street Journal*

(More Graphs on Page C1.)

Toyota, striking it at approximately 2:32 p.m. Pacific Standard Time. At impact, radar guns clocked the President at 27 miles per hour.

President Clinton had just finished a short impromptu speech at Caffe Roma, a local coffeehouse frequented by tattoo artisans, students, and people of uncertain employment. As he posed "pulling a latte" for photographers, he spied some local youth "street luging" on the hill outside. Apparently in an effort to energize the well-caffeinated but still-indolent crowd, off he went.

Onlookers said that Clinton had some difficulty convincing the youngsters to let him try. "You know, I was rebellious when I was younger, just like you." Clinton then donned a wool cap sporting the emblem "Wu Tang", but the young *slackier* remained unimpressed until the President revealed his pierced nipple, a souveneir from Oxford.

Street luge, an urban cousin of the Olympic event, is one of several so-called "extreme sports" popular with today's youth and glamorized by frequent exposure on MTV and ESPN, two cult cable channels. James Lofton, of the Washington; D.C.–based Brookings Institute, said, "Extreme sports are essentially the suicide attempt reborn as recreation." He added that most extreme sports involve equipment "originally created for the space program, and nearly as expensive."

Political observers saw the President's painful stunt as an attempt to continue his successful 1996 campaign—throughout his entire second term "or longer, if necessary." Among 18- to 24-year-olds, the President finished a worrisome second, behind perennial fourth- or fifth-party candidate Lenora Fulani "because she has a cool name."

However, the cynical denizens of Seattle's Capitol Hill neighborhood, the veritable cradle of slackerdom, were unimpressed by Clinton's attempt. "He looked stiff on the board, like a mounted fish," said "The Remora," a freelance hemp merchant and sometime student at Cornish College of the Arts, just up the road from the crash site. "If he grew a soul patch [a variant of goatee nesting between

Please Turn to Page A8, Column 1

rats, and they won't tell us where they buried them," a disgruntled Daly official said. "My dog's locked in there, and he's probably crapping all over the place."

* * *

NASA announced that the microorganisms discovered on a Martian meteor perished as a result of a heavy tax burden coupled with a bloated, meddlesome bureaucracy. "Let it be a lesson to us all," said Dr. Wayne Aspirin, Chief Economist for NASA. Aspirin would not comment on whether markets free enough to sustain life exist outside this solar system.

* * *

In a controversial move, the Federal Reserve Board plans to cut the lending rate to zero today in an effort to spur a lagging economy. "Go to it, fellas!" read a press release to be issued this morning. "Last one to 30% growth is a rotten egg!"

* * *

A group of former editors are suing their ex-boss, Time-Life style maven Martha Stuart. The suit, asking for damages of $50 million, says that Ms. Stuart caused "grave psychological damage" by holding editorial meetings while defecating. "Ahh, everybody does that," said Reginald Bismuth-Lewis, a spokesperson for Ms. Stuart.

* * *

Markets—

Stocks: Volume 7 shares. Dow Jones Industrials 6050.04 up 982. Hurrah!

Bonds: Lehman Brothers Treasury index 14.05, off 1023. (*Whew.* If you're in bonds, go have a drink on the Club car.)

Commodities: Baby Oil $1.49 a pint, up .003. Dow Jones futures index 175.43 up 2. Dow Jones grasshopper head futures index 12012.52, up 11030.

Dollar: three Hershey kisses and a dollar equals 100 yen, up from two M&Ms; 1900 pesos and a Mexican toddler, up from a bird.

best of 'em," he said in a press release. The 63-year-old hopes to encourage illiterates in the banking and investment communities to come forward and seek help. "It gudd he do," said an industry analyst. (Article on Page A2.)

* * *

The embattled Edison Project announced "a last-ditch effort to get kids interested in history"—a hyper-violent video game called *Live Free or DIE!*. This game pits great figures from American history against each other in a futuristic, kung-fu flavored fight to the death. CEO Benno Schmidt, once an educational figure of some importance, delighted the press by demonstrating how William Jennings Bryan can rip an opponent's spine out "by force of oratory alone!"

* * *

Frenchy scientists announced that common species of spiders wear hats, and the usually-sleepy American haberdashery industry is abuzz. "We could get 400 cowboy hats from a single piece of felt," said Giacomo Stetson, of Stetson Hats. "Some of our salespeople are a little squeamish," said a spokesperson for Kangol, "but we feel that after the training program, they'll realize that spiders are just like anybody else." (Article on Page B1.)

* * *

The latest Beltway bombshell is—believe it or not—a slavery scandal. When 500 Washington politicians, lobbyists and journalists were surveyed by recent Gallup poll, 62% of them agreed with the statement, "I own slaves." "Frankly, I think they're all sitting on a political volcano," said one insider. Columnist George Will, owner of Matthew, Karen, and James, disagrees. "I guess slavery is no longer *politically correct*," he snorted. "The American people have always been envious of their masters, and of me in particular."

* * *

The American Association of Editors released new guidelines on the identification of sources. From now on "off the record" will mean that the person being quoted was whispering, and sources quoted "on deep background" will have to stand behind reporters when they talk.

Eudora Limpet & Pepper

markets from Tokyo to Caracas tremble in anticipation. Because, as Mr. Louis Grimm, a broker with Golden Sacs in San Francisco, says, "This cat is the greatest financial genius since Adam Smith. Possibly greater."

Pepper picks stocks. And Pepper, it seems, has never made a mistake. Ever.

How can an animal with an estimated IQ of 29 outperform the Dow Jones by 3,152 percent over a five-year period? Mrs. Limpet, herself no genius, is at a loss to explain it all. "Pepper was a perfectly normal cat — yarn, mice, milk, hairballs, the usual. Maybe even on the dim side — he never could even figure out the toy mouse I bought him years ago. But one day, I had spread out some stock certificates on the kitchen table — my eyesight isn't what it used to be, and I had mistaken them for playing cards — when he jumped up, sat down on one and wouldn't get up."

What the kindly old Mrs. Limpet didn't know is that her feline had taken his morning nap on 50 shares of Flapjack Pharmaceuticals, which was that very day to become the takeover target of British leveraged-buyout artist Sir Buckminster Squeam (Squeam has since filed a $39 million lawsuit against Pepper, claiming the kitty had inside knowledge of his planned takeover. "Said animal had probably spoken to Mr. Squeam's feline Monroe in an illegal attempt to subvert the world financial system," he has claimed in a deposition filed in London).

When the white-haired septuagenarian mentioned Pepper's behavior in passing

Please Turn to Page A3, Column 5

TODAY'S CONTENTS

SORRY IT'S SMALL—WE'VE BEEN SICK

THREE SECTIONS

INDUSTRY FOCUS

DEAD BODIES: Corpses, long considered useless and icky, have proven to be a source of profit, profit, PROFIT! **Page B1.**

MEDICINE: Lilly scientists reveal that addition of Prozac makes plants grow sideways, **A4**.

WHO'S NEWS: CEO, after a brush with death, finds family overrated, more fulfillment in work, **B2**.

PUBLISHING: Recent deluge of parodies render normal magazines meaningless, **B3**.

POLITICS & POLICY: Bizarre loophole in regulation makes cows, bees fill out tax forms, **A8.**

INTERNATIONAL: China announces plans to stick a fiber-optic cable in back of every citizen's head, **B4.**

LEISURE & ARTS: "Poop Dreams," guano documentary, is reviewed, **A5.**

FOREIGN MARKETS: Nikkei plummets due to South Korean curse, **C2.**

grasshopper heads are allowed in a pound of corn meal: from seven heads to ten billion. "It's obvious they bowed to political pressure," says one disgruntled Agriculture employee. "The grasshopper head lobby is stronger than you think." The Department is also promulgating peculiar new standards where none existed before, including nine praying mantis legs per hamburger, one-half boll weevil per walnut, and seven hundred scorpions per orange.

Grasshopper head futures at the Chicago Board of Trade skyrocketed nearly 4,000% yesterday.

MONEY TALKS in Washington, but something else talks even louder: backrubs.

"It's well known that Dick Gephardt will vote any way you want if you have 'the talented hands,'" said one lobbyist. "He rubs up against you like a cat and purrs." But love of the rub knows no party: GOP honcho Richard Armey is rumored to have changed a recent vote because the Saudi ambassador came over to his house the night before to rub his back.

The backrub craze has created new opportunities for lobbyists. If a legislator wakes up in the middle of the night with a bad dream, Lockheed lobbyists will let congressmen sleep in their beds with them, and will even sing them "Kumbaya"; most shocking, representatives of embattled Archer Daniel Midlands sometimes write them notes so that they can stay home from Congress—*even if they're not really sick.*

DOG DAYS: Undersecretary of State for East Asia Franklin Emory sparked controversy yesterday by suggesting the U.S. should declare war on China "because they eat puppy dogs." In a speech at Harvard University, Emory said that "China is currently laying plans to invade the United States and seize our rich canine resources. ...Pretty soon old Deng will be stretched out on Venice Beach looking at the ladies and eating Lassie a la King."

Secretary of State Madeline Albright quickly disavowed Emory's speech.

"What really gets my blood boiling," stated Albright, *"is the Persians. They use their hand to wipe their butt!"*

A CIA OFFICIAL said that Bill Clinton has been a victim of mindcontrol since 1995. "A rogue element of the VFW abducted the President after a speech in Omaha, and re-programmed his brain to act like a Republican." Since the brainwashed "Nebraskan Candidate" won handily, "we assume that the plan backfired." The White House said Clinton has no plans to seek therapy for his condition. "If it ain't broke, don't fix it—anyway, HRC likes it."

over the company's poor performance resulted in an kamikazoid restructuring plan; since 1991, the company has been making steady, if painful, progress towards its twin goals of paring staff down to the bone, and squeezing the absolute maximum efficiency from its physical plant.

The complete lack of activity, which lends a slightly ghost town-like feeling to offices which once bustled, would make one believe that Webster was a company on the ropes. Not so — its stock, listed on the Nasdaq, has posted a 230% rise since June, on the strength of massive employee layoffs. So massive, in fact, that there is no one left to run the company.

The final straw, "the final piece in the puzzle," came yesterday, when Webster CEO Neil F. Jordan, who had presided over the company's efforts to regain profitability, summarily fired President Quinn Daloit, and, in a brutal bit of business harikiri, himself. "...and don't come back!" He told himself in a press release.

Webster's stock leaped at the news that the company had voluntarily imploded. As of yesterday's close, Webster Technology's stock stood at 78 3/4, up 117% from the previous day's trading. It remains to be seen whether this immediate proof of Jordan's acumen will solidify into permanent gains for Webster, but most observers are confident. "There's no one there," said an industry executive. "Who's gonna do anything?"

"In the past, Webster was in a lot of businesses we shouldn't have been in, like water-purification," said Jordan, in a statement released yesterday afternoon. "Over the past several years, we here at Webster have worked hard to scale back, to concentrate on only those areas where we can compete effectively. The question is: what can Webster do best? And the answer is: nothing. *Absolutely nothing.*

"Through spit, grit, and hard work, we have reached our goal. Goodbye."

Competitors have taken notice of Webster's meteoric rise. Daniel Grady, President of BTI, Webster's main competitor, said, "For years, we've been playing the fool for Webster's schemes — they'd lay off twenty or so people, we'd hire them and expand our operations. Meanwhile, we were having a harder and harder time keeping up." BTI has been steadily losing market share to Webster as the latter bled itself white; the two companies have abruptly switched places, when BTI had a commanding 64% share as late as May 1994, before Webster's lemming-like plan began in earnest. After yesterday's coup de grace, rumors

Please Tu n to Page A3, Column 6

NATIONAL

Fed Chair Sez: "So Long, Suckers! See You in 3,000 Years!"

A Jubilant Greenspan Throws in Towel, Gets Frozen In Block of Ice

By ELLE SEGUNDO

Staff Reporter of THE BULL STREET JOURNAL

NEW YORK—Claiming that uncertain economic times have made his life too difficult to bear, Federal Reserve Chairman Alan Greenspan is having himself put into suspended animation until America has found a cure for its monetary instability.

"I'm nervous as hell and I can't take it anymore," says Greenspan. "If unemployment goes down, inflation goes up. If the stock market goes up, the bond market goes down. And as Fed chairman, I am powerless to affect it in any way. For all the big titles and impressive economic mumbo-jumbo, I'm along for the ride, just like any other rube!"

But rather than check out for good,

Greenspan is going the Walt Disney route. Working with top scientists, Greenspan is having himself placed in cryogenic deep-freeze. His body will be perfectly preserved until a special sensor, tied into a Wall Street mainframe computer, reads that the Dow Jones industrial average has topped the 20,000 mark. "Then I will be woken up, well rested and ready to run the economy in those distant, headier times."

Experts believe that the Dow may not reach this point for 10,000 years, but Greenspan is nonplussed by the changes that may take place by then. "Look at the Neanderthals recently discovered frozen in the Alps," he says. "They look like pretty sharp cookies to me." Greenspan is also looking forward to cures for can-

cer, AIDS, and his perpetual grimace.

Markets were volatile upon hearing the news that the nation's top economist was heading into deep freeze rather than face America's economic problems, with the Dow off 810 points in frenzied, panicked trading. Greenspan, however, couldn't care less. "I'll be in my dollar-bill jammies, sleeping like a baby. So long, you losers!"

Housing Starts Up, But Most Are Ugly, Tacky

The government released statistics for July, which revealed that housing starts were up 1.5%, suggesting that the economy continued to be robust. However, in an uncommon bit of subjective judgement, the report said that "most of these new houses are really horrible-looking."

The report also raised some question as to how many of these housing starts would be completed: "It's no big deal to start a house *Anybody* can start a house—but how many people finish them? Our advice: don't brag so much."

As a result, the positive news did not buoy the markets as could have been expected.

Tycoon Tyke Slapped With "Spiking" Charges

By KERMIT LeFROG

Staff Reporter of THE BULL STREET JOURNAL

PHOENIX—An attorney for Lewis Mayer, the business legend who turned a $2.50 investment into a chain of 370 kool-aid stands across the Southwest, acknowledged yesterday that he is under Federal investigation for spiking his product. Damning company memos gathered in a six-month sting operation reveal that Mayer, at just eight the youngest self-made millionaire in United States history, encouraged his stands to spike their wares with "codeine, vodka and pee-pee...[T]his last one won't help you sell more units, but it is really funny."

According to an obscure Arizona law, selling kool-aid with urine in it carries a minimum sentence of three years.

The lawsuit comes at a bad time for Mayer, which is battling unseasonably cool weather as well as its employees' continuing inability to count and make change. Industry observers suggest that the lawsuit will likely scuttle the long-

rumored deal with soft-drink giant Coca-Cola to take over the $50 million a year business.

. The kool-aid tycoon, an idol to fledgling businesspeople everywhere, is no stranger to controversy. The investigation comes on the heels of several lawsuits filed last summer, after six customers went blind from drinking wood alcohol at a Mayer stand in Tempe.

The company's nine year old general counsel, Francis Glick, read a statement from Mr. Mayer. "I resent the insinuation that my competitive advantage has stemmed from the use of addictive substances. I built Mayer the old-fashioned way—offering a better product at a competitive price, putting the customer first, and keeping ants out of the drink mix...That having been said, I have no idea what our franchisees are doing. You have to understand, they're five and six years old. Most of them can't even keep their fingers out of their noses."

Stocks Sluggish as Traders Lose Interest

NYSE Floor Degenerates, Hosts First Ever Games of Four-Square, Dodge Ball and Duck-Duck-Goose

By FRANKLIN PIERCED

Staff Reporter of THE BULL STREET JOURNAL

NEW YORK—In a strange display of mass hysteria virtually unduplicated in American financial history, the trading floor of the New York Stock Exchange became a playground this afternoon. One stressed-out trader after another swapped their Tums for Pez and played kids' games. Later, it got dark and they had to go in for supper.

Exuberant sessions of duck-duck-goose and capture the flag began to be improvised "sometime after 1:30." Burbling, bull-market like glee quickly spread around the floor, and by 1:47—when someone abruptly kicked out the plug— all adult financial activities had ceased. All of the world's major financial markets reported crank phone calls at or around this time, which ceased only after taking their phones off the hook.

The pandemonium reached its high-point about 2:45, when unidentified individuals brought five partially-inflated playground-style "red balls" into the Exchange. Sources say that dodge ball and four-square games were then hastily organized. Some traders reported slight injuries; however, all disputes were

settled with a minimum of tears.

At 3:17, the Big Board was made to read "Guy Walters is the best!!!" over and over, thanks to a simple computer program. This continued for the rest of the day. Meanies plan to question Guy Walters in connection with the incident, but he says it wasn't him that did it.

Ahh...Pie!

The Gentleman's Reward

After a gritty day, there's nothing like sliding one of our huge, thick pies into a hot, hot oven. When was the last time you did it? Had pie? Whether it was yesterday or two years ago, we'll bet *you remember.* The sounds. The smells. The anticipation.

And then...it's done. Until the next time.

It satisfies something deep within you—because underneath the well-groomed exterior, you're a pie-eater, an *animal.* Impress an important client, or give yourself a treat far away from home. It's time you experienced the excitement...the enticement...the ecstasy, again. Of pie.

Genuine Nebraska Pie Co.

1-900-HOT-PIE

24 hrs/7 days • We cater "Parties" • All pies between 18-22

Our cheerful, experienced, only slightly married operators are
waiting to
SATISFY YOUR CRAVINGS!

Adults only, please— under 18, please lie to parents before you call.
Mention this ad and get a FREE MASSAGE

Tracking the Economy

Monday: Seattle, WA, where it speaks at a private luncheon for Microsoft executives.

Tuesday: outside Fonda, IA, until driven away by angry, rock-throwing mob of farmers.

Wednesday: spotted in Baldwin, MO—dismissed by officials as "a weather balloon."

Unofficial plans are afoot to have "play day" every other Friday— NYSE officials refused to comment. Meanwhile, President Clinton reassured a jittery public, that— perhaps for the first time— questioned the sanity of the professionals managing the late great President Herbert Hoover, he said, "Don't worry, everything's under complete control!"

Look at Ozymandias.

Yes, it's true—
here at Ozymandias, we don't have a "tradition."
We don't have any "distinguished alumni."
We don't have a "world-class faculty."
More to the point, we don't have "anyone."

You see, at Ozymandias, we don't have even the most rudimentary "campus."

That's because we don't have the most cutting-edge "facilities."

If you enroll here, there won't be any "place" that you can "go."

Because we don't believe in teaching students "things."
We don't believe in the "concept" of "learning."
We don't believe in giving you a "degree."
Most important, we don't believe in the "reality" of your "existence."

Do you?

WE DON'T.

OZYMANDIAS UNIVERSITY M.B.A. PROGRAM*

---

as "a weather balloon."
Thursday: Los Angeles, CA, where it waits tables for a day while waiting for its big break.
Friday: Shenzhen Province, People's Republic of China. Economy has "no plans to return."

Financier Rohatyn Spells Out Illiteracy

NEW YORK— In a stunning press release, high-flying New York financier Felix G. Rohatyn, admitted that he didn't know how to read. "Never did," said the statement, whose frequent grammatical *cul-de-sacs* and maddening misspellings, added mute testimony to Rohatyn's plight. "I got through college on a football scholarship."

The banker, thought by some to be the premier authority regarding corporate take-overs, has enjoyed universal esteem in the financial community since helping rescue New York from bankruptcy in the mid-1970s.

"I'm tired of the lies, of the outrageous deceit— of faking my way through meetings, then running to the john to puzzle out a few key phrases," Rohatyn wrote. "I think it says something about this country that someone could rise to the level I have, and had no idea how to read. Trouble is, I have no idea what it says. Particularly if you write it down."

A source in the Federal Reserve, where Rohatyn currently occupies the number two spot, predicted his imminent dismissal, saying, "You have to admire his candor and courage— however; admiring someone and keeping them on the payroll are two totally separate issues."

CORRECTIONS & AMPLIFICATIONS

WORKERS earning less than $20,000 per year are estimated at 72,500,000, not 13,250, as reported in the Feb. 14 *Journal.* The inability of the editors to believe in this figure caused the error.

* * *

The scandal referred to as Watergate was the attempted cover-up of a bungled burglary at the Democratic national headquarters. It was NOT, as stated in an August 9, 1974 article, a "War-of-the-Worlds-like hoax perpetrated by *The Washington Post* in an effort to spur its miniscule circulation." Sorry it took us so long.

* * *

Yesterday's NYSE close was reported to be -32,002.89, due to a freak transposition. The *Journal* regrets the subsequent collapse of the American economy.

* * *

PRESIDENT CLINTON does not eat babies. An article Friday incorrectly stated that he eats babies "all the time—breakfast, lunch and dinner." In his speech to a Madison, Wisconsin high school, the President called children "the hope of Tomorrow" and not "as addictive as potato chips."

* * *

APPLE COMPUTER is not experimenting with the sexual preference of the operating system on its Macintosh line of personal computers. An article in Thursday's *Journal* reported that "Sometime in 1997, Apple plans to release a special gay OS, code-named 'Garland'." We have no idea how this got in the paper, but we believe the temp currently employed as Executive Editor is responsible.

* * *

IN THURSDAY'S special report on Welfare reform. Gloria Jackson was misidentified as "a Caddy-drivin' Welfare Queen game show-watchin' lima bean," instead of "a 16 year old mother of three, holding down two minimum-wage jobs, trying not to get shot." The *Journal* regrets Ms. Jackson subsequent loss of said jobs, and national demonization as "everything that has gone wrong in this country since 1968." Hang in there, Gloria.

READER'S NOTES

This space compliments of
THE BULL STREET JOURNAL PARODY

New Chinese Stock Market Deals in Chinese

Human Rights Violations Are Like Potato Chips—
After the First One, It's Impossible to Stop

BY STARRE CHILD
Staff Reporter of THE BULL STREET JOURNAL.

BEIJING— In a move sure to anger human-rights groups already irked with China's treatment of its citizens, one of the country's most pathologically busting provinces has created a stock market offering shares in, of all things, people. According to Hunanese officials, this is an attempt to transfer some of China's growing wealth from the urban elite, to the masses from the countryside. These cash-poor peasants, called "*bao de*" or "dipsticks," have largely been left behind as the country busily turns itself into one big Times Square of Asia.

"We believe that placing yourself on the The Glorious Human Human Stock Exchange of the People will allow, you to raise capital more easily, with reduced risk to investors," said Gao Gang, the silver-haired, no-nonsense head of the GHHSE (pronounced "geeze.') The spanking new bourse, he proudly notes, has several desktop computers and is the only one of its kind to have a state-of-the-art jail in the bottom. (The structure was built by a German company, under the impression that it was to be a "maximum security hotel for foreigners.")

Gao summarily dismissed any possible criticisms as the "piteous malingering of a few freedom-crazed Westerners," who are just jealous that they didn't think of it first. "It's not slavery," said Gao. "Far, far from it." But when presented with a definition of "slavery," Gao replied. "Oh.

Then it *is* slavery.

"However, what you call in the West call 'slavery,' we call 'extremely directed activities.'"

For a small fee, Chinese nationals will be allowed to list themselves on the Ex-

well, it is likely that overseas Chinese will also be listed in the near future. The eventual listing of Taiwanese without telling them seems almost certain.

"Our main concern is, what if someone owns 51% of you, and you're a lousy

> 'It's not slavery,' said a Chinese official. 'Far, far from it.' But when presented with a definition of "slavery," the official coolly replied, 'Oh. Then it *is* slavery.
>
> 'However, what you in the West call "slavery," we call "extremely directed activity."[…]Let us now talk about the US' high rate of crime-ing, and how mean you were to Martin Luther King.'

change, after undergoing a rigorous physical and mental examination, so that State may verify information contained in their prospectus. Exchange officials will then set an opening price according to the individual's skills, health and overall earning potential; preferred and common shares will be available, and dividends will be offered at the discretion of an independent observer affiliated with the GHHSE. Presently, only Chinese citizens can list themselves on the Exchange, but if the experiment goes

investment?" said Lynn Johnston, spokesman for Free! Free! Free!, a human rights organization based in Toronto. "Do you liquidate yourself?"

"So what if you did? What's the big deal? Japanese have been doing that for centuries," said Lin Gaofeng, a spokesman for Xinhua, the New China News Agency. "You don't hear any Chinese people complaining, do you? Shut up! That was you talking behind your hand! Get out of here! Give me your wallet!"

A *German* Firm's New Gene-Splicing Toy Fuels Protests

BY FINGER PRINCE
Staff Reporter of THE BULL STREET JOURNAL

Several international human rights groups have lodged a protest with the World Court in The Hague over the arrival on store shelves of the first gene-splicing kit available for home use. The strongly worded statement from Amnesty International, Medicins sans Frontières, and Leave My Genes Alone!, claims that [German needed] (loosely translated as 'People's Home Ethnic Purity Plaything) "is an attempt to renew the horrific 'master race' policies of the Nazi regime."

Kindermachen AG of Frankfurt, replied in a press release that "our kit allows parents to explore the wonders of their own DNA…To allege that our $99.99 product has anything in common with certain undertakings earlier this century is preposterous and libelous (or slanderous, whichever is appropriate)."

While Kindermachen has admitted using data from Nazi experiments, the press release holds that the company only utilized experiments done on chickpeas. "While no one is minimizing what chickpeas endured under the Nazi regime, we believe that the enjoyment of consumers today is at least as important as remembering the sacrifices and shames of yesteryear."

A company spokesperson in Frankfurt had no additional comment, but, when read the above statement, would only say, "Who wrote *that?*"

The kit contains a small centrifuge, a microscope, some glass slides, a superfine scalpel, and some vegetable dye for marking chromosomes. Using an enclosed partial map of the human genome, buyers can pinpoint the location of characteristics such as hair color, eye color, and intelligence. Though the outside of the kit warns that "attempting to alter chromosomes is dangerous and difficult," a list of "Fun Experiments!" includes:

• "try to change the hair color of your animal [sic] to blue, and back again in under 30 days"

• "add a second set of eyes to a frog"

• "change the color of black ants to white, and then eliminate all non-white ants in three months,"

Crafty Western Consumer Goods Companies Turn Third-World Ignorance Into Big Profits

VINDALOO, INDIA— Devi Batimella likes putting toothpaste in her armpits. The more she sweats, the more it foams —"It makes my clothes smell minty," she says. "It also helps control tartar." Meanwhile, Ms. Batimella cannot leave her house, thanks to a profusion of marriage proposals that often turn violent when she so much as appears at a front window. Her lawn is crowded with suitors, chanting her name and engaging in

vorite dipping sauce for chicken wings (another bit of Western culture recently taken to heart) in Hanoi's top restaurants? Dandruff shampoo.

Unlike other, more conventional companies, the idea of novel uses is one that Prater & Grimmle welcomes. "We're not here to tell you 'do this, don't do that' with our products," said Prater President Janet Acheson. "Each culture— not to mention each customer— has their own

compete with cheap, low quality Russian goods (mostly Soviet-era Army surplus), but also worthless natural remedies that have been used for centuries. Effectiveness can run a distant second to tradition, more often than efficiency-mad Westerners might think.

P&G's method of tying use of its products to eternal salvation has paid dividends. "We take some little-known God or Goddess from a target religion, and

Pepper Licks Paws and the Market

Continued From First Page

to her son-in-law Albert Loam —"a pig-eyed stockbroker. not to mention a dog person" — he had already heard about the Flapjack takeover bid. With a wife, two mistresses, and a 60 percent stake in a failing string of discount nursing homes, Loam needed a big score. He decided to test Pepper's prognostications by bringing over some more stock notes and spread them out in the living room.

"He prowled around and plunked himself down on Yspilanti Aluminum, not knowing, of course, that in two days a YP scientist would patent a way of using aluminum to keep third world children from starving," says Loam. He intended to keep the news a secret, but one of his girlfriends overheard Loam writing about Pepper's abilities in this journal. ("He has to speak every word he writes because he's so stupid," says Mrs. Limpet. "My daughter is, and has always been, out of her mind." For his part, Loam calls his mother-in-law "a withered old hag whose cat I love very much.") This girlfriend, in order to spite Loam, called Nightly Business Report, and the word — or the *purr* — was out.

Soon, dozens of brokers were visiting the Limpet residence, to see for themselves this miracle in action. "They brought all sorts of things — stock certificates, the financial pages of newspapers, annual reports, even company softball team uniforms" Mrs. Limpet says. Whatever medium was used, Pepper, through various combinations of sniffing, scratching, and urinating, would make his choice clear. The dowager of Happy Lane didn't know what to make of it all, but rejected all offers to buy the cat. "First, they offered me all sorts of outrageous amounts," she says, "but when an old lady loses her last cat, it's like getting a notice from the Grim Reaper: 'see you soon.' Then these nice young men told me they just wanted a hair or blood sample."

Limpet tried to chase them off by waving her support hose, but the brokers had brought lint brushes and took approximately 30 pounds of cat hair to the Laboratory for Genetic Research in Faint Harbor, New York, where the best scientific minds in the world spend three years and 176 million dollars trying to clone Pepper so that a small number of white men

ability of a cat to select stocks in a seemingly random fashion that brutally outperforms any choices made by human stockbrokers with years of training and six-figure incomes seems to imply that picking stocks has nothing to do with skill or ability. "Nothing could be further from the truth," says Thomas Hang, partner at Bare Sterns in Greenwich. "Our brokers deserve every cent they make. But just to make sure the public doesn't get the wrong message, we've hired the public relations firm of Hale & Notlob to get the word out."

The first results of H & N's work will be seen this weekend with full-page ads in the New York *Times* reading. "There's nothing wrong with the 'miracle cat'! But America's brokerages want to remind you that the last place where so much trust was put in an animal was Communist North Korea and their famous Laughing Horse, which was a fake!"

The greater dilemma facing this country is that Pepper, at 22 years of age, will not live forever. With the world's financial markets hanging on his every hairball, his death would cause calamitous uncertainty, quite possibility triggering a depression. The level of concern in Washington could be seen last month when Pepper had a brief epileptic fit, prompting Federal Reserve Chairman Alan Greenspan to declare, "I have just spoken with Pepper's veterinarian. The cat is fine. Repeat: THE CAT IS FINE." Politicians of both parties sent their best regards to Mrs. Limpet's house, and President Clinton's cat Socks was said to be "very concerned."

Again, science and industry have not been idle in trying to extend Pepper's life. Seventy cans of high-protein, low-fat cat food, each costing $100,000 and requiring two years to make, have been sent to Ampersand *gratis*. J. Walter Fluke of the Institute for Genetic Research says, "Our specially-formulated diet will guarantee that Pepper will live for three billion years, or until the Sun explodes. And at that point, what happens to the stock market won't matter." But Bare Sterns' Hang isn't convinced. "Without a fully-functioning stock market, humanity will never survive the end of the universe. Long live Pepper the cat!"

_____

Webster's Message:

ers, chanting her name and engaging in

By Bull Street Journal staff reporters Piper "Pep" Chardray in Greenwich, and Peter Sandwedge somewhere south of the Equator, with additional research by that guy Peter met in a bar in New Delhi who swears it's all true "on a stack of Bibles or Bhagvad-Gitas or whatever."

tests of physical strength to impress her— but just six months ago, it seemed unlikely that Ms. Batimella would ever be married. "I was uglier than a dog's dinner. I owe all of my new popularity to Sparkly," she beams.

Consumer-products giant **Prater and Grimmle** couldn't be happier either. Prater is basking in a torrent of sales from so-called Third World regions, as its products make inroads with a new, unsophisticated group of customers. Many of whom use a bevy of name brands familiar to Westerners in ways that range from the merely bizarre to the downright dangerous.

Toothpaste in the armpits in only the tip of the iceberg. In Thailand, no self-respecting member of the *haute monde* would be seen without cotton swabs dangling from their nose and ears. Pine-scented disinfectant is the perfume of choice in Sri Lanka. And what's the fa-

mention each customer— has their own needs, and we think telling them not to swab detergent in their eyes, is frankly a little paternalistic." P&G now has a team of seven people thinking up wacky uses for their products. "All we ask is that nobody with access to a lawyer gets permanently injured," says Barry Brannigan, P&G's head of New Use Development. "Otherwise, just think of any way somebody could use a *lot* of product. Like sealing your driveway with hair gel. That's a good one."

P&G looks to the many new uses ever so gently suggested by baking soda companies during the 70's and 80's, as a textbook case of how to revitalize a mature product. Fred Carlin, a marketing consultant, agrees. "In a few short years, baking soda changed from a old-fashioned, back-of-the-cupboard kitchen ingredient, to the centerpiece of any young, with-it refrigerator."

Prater & Grimmle's aggressive policy is not universal in the industry: Belle Cosmetics decided to pull its popular Softee line of hand lotions in 1994, after it was widely publicized that customers were using it as a contraceptive *and* as salad dressing, often at the same time.

Of course, the real story is not what P&G's consumers are using the products for, but that they are using the products at all. Western toiletries not only have to

or Goddess from a target religion, and make him our spokesman," said Acheson. "It may be blasphemous, but it's highly cost-effective." Plus, there is a tremendous amount of built-in name recognition. "It's like, 'Hey, that's the baby powder Shriketh, Eater of Worlds uses!'" said David Plant, Prater and Grimmle's representative for Bhutan. "Where real estate and labor are cheap enough, we have already begun to build actual churches to selected products." He adds that sacred-style imagery is particularly effective in moving product in areas of low literacy.

Predictably, some people are less than thrilled at Western companies co-opting their religious figures to "sell more units." "I, for one, am offended when Dodi, the Enigmatic Martyr, appears in the paper hawking pens," fumed Sandhi Jodphur, a leading intellectual and fuddy-duddy. But most people don't seem to mind. "I think it turns our Gods and Goddesses into people that the kids can relate to, that have problems just like them," said Div Dellib, a teacher in Calcutta. "They can say, 'This is Smoothy, the pimple cream Prince Rondiponton was using during his race with the Moon. If the Divine Prince had a bad complexion, and still married the Butterfly Consort, I shouldn't get so down."

Cheaters Never Prosper, You Know

Good-for-Ø Foreign·Companies Turning to Espionage

By Jesus C. Superstar
Stiff Reporter of The Bull Street Journal

Microsoft veterans call the winding, tree-shaded road outside Building 26 "Crow's Walk." It's a grisly tribute to the birds who pluck their dinner from the heads, impaled on stakes every ten feet or so, all the way up the hill.

"It gets your attention, just like it's supposed to," says Denise Bilcher of Microsoft's public relations department. "If you're not doing anything wrong, you have nothing to worry about."

The heads, trophies of the company's war on industrial espionage, have been going up with ever-increasing frequency. Though no Microsoft employees will elaborate, it is widely acknowledged these "nameless drifters" are employed by Europe's beleagured computer industry. Spies have been flooding Microsoft and other leading American computer manufacturers since the early 90's. Soon, space on the hill will be a problem.

"You can spot foreign spies pretty easily," said the head of security for a major Silicon Valley infotech firm. "They're the ones who talk funny."

Once caught, treatment of spies varies from company to company— new employees would be wise to read through their orientation packet. Not all companies are legally savvy enough to get away with summary executions, like Microsoft. "At Lotus, we have to conduct elaborate show trials first, or the police will get mad," said an official. "Usually, we just 'snip 'em' and let 'em go," says a guard at Silicon Graphics, referring to the blanket castration policy put in place in late 1994. Others use subtle brain-washing techniques dating back to the Korean War.

Luckily for the industry, experts believe that the quality of information getting through to foreign competitors is low. Microsoft released an intercepted fax, sent by an infiltrator posing as a vending machine stocker: "X-13 reporting in. Have made lean-to in bushes near campus. Everyone has a special palm-sized button, which they move around; perhaps it is a nervous habit brought on by the constant monitoring, or maybe a wrist-relieving exercise…What they call 'Windows 95' is a special kind of screen-saver…Guards here are doughy-soft and stupid. Must go, someone's coming…I guess it was just the air-conditioner. As I was—GAK!"

European companies deny stealing secrets with numbing regularity. "Any of our new products could blow your Mac Pluses out of the water," said an indignant Jacques LeJacques, head of France's Le Groupe Cow. "Our BASIC programmings are the best in the world, and our newest chips execute six instructions a second. Stealing? To that, I say a hearty 'Piffle!'"

However, few doubt that the lying Frenchies would scramble for any advantage in this most competitive of industries. With the Cold War over, there's no shortage of ex-spies hungrily scouring Europe and Asia for business clients. Sources say that officials from our own CIA check Microsoft's "Crow's Walk" regularly, identifying ex-agents through dental records.

ants in three months."

Leave Our Genes Alone! president Alfred Lobe is horrified at what he calls the "blithe lack of irony" being practiced by Kindermachen. "They're taking the darkest chapter of ignorance and evil in human history and repackaging it for fun and profit. As the saying goes, 'Those who forget the past are doomed to repeat it.'"

Particularly irksome to LOGA! has been the co-sponsorship of children's toy giant Playskool in marketing the kit to young children. Called "My First Home Eugenics Kit," the device substitutes plastic slides for glass and a powerful laser for the enclosed scalpel, lasers being less likely to put out an eye. The kit also warns parents that they may want to supervise their children's use of the toy, since any mutations accidentally introduced into the youngster's body will affect the parent's descendants forever.

Indeed, Playskool, riding a crest of success from its new "real world toy line" —which includes "My First Beeper," "My First Lawsuit," and, only last month, "My First Admission of Carrying Out Horrible Experiments"—practically invites children to alter their family's genetic makeup. The abovementioned experiments ask kids to compare their parents to "people you see on TV and in magazines" and to "list 10 ways your parents could be more like them." Though the kit does not suggest actually altering the user's own genes, LOGA!'s Lobe says that it is not difficult for children to make the necessary connections. "Kids are smart," he says. "Mine have locked me out of my house for years."

However, J. Walter Fluke, of the Laboratory for Genetic Research in Faint Harbor, New York, says that it is impossible for the user of a $100 kit to make complicated changes in human DNA. "We've been working for 14 years and have spent over $1 billion on trying to alter DNA and have achieved shinola." When asked how recent advances in isolating the most basic building blocks of life outside of the cell might affect the future of mankind, Fluke added, "What's a *cell*?"

LOGA! has been calling for a boycott of all Kindermachen products. This is expected not to be very effective, since besides the eugenics kit, the beleagured Kindermachen's only other product is a faultering line of designer lingerie manufactued in Romania. The World Court has scheduled preliminary hearings for next week, pending the conclusion of a case brought by a flock of migratory egrets suing the government of Myanmar for "various offenses."

could make huge amounts of money in the world stock markets. "Just what science was meant to do," says Project Kitty Klone director J. Walter Fluke. "Though we were unsuccessful in pleasing our masters, we did have some technological spin-offs which will benefit all of mankind." He cites the discovery of the gene which causes cats to play with yarn. "Imagine the possibilities!"

Unfortunately for the old battle-ax, where millions of dollars are at stake, capitalism can be relentless in is pursuit of profits. Unable to figure out the scientific basis for Pepper's prognostications, brokerage houses are sparing no expense in trying to get the Wonder Kitty to sit on their stock and send its value through the roof. Limpet has been sent stock certificates printed on paper specially treated with pheromones and catnip, or covered with pictures of mice. "The worst was a Dutch firm which placed a tiny superpowerful magnet in one stock certificate and attempted to feed Pepper shotgun pellets in his food," says Limpet. "Not only did Pepper avoid their food, but the magnet tore my artificial hip out of my body from 75 feet away."

The latest technology has been utilized to keep track of Pepper's movements and detect where the cat has sat down before the frumpy crone makes her twice-daily announcement of his stock choices. Every day, helicopters equipped with the Pentagon's most sensitive infrared cameras fill the airspace above Limpet's house, following the cat's every movements. Of course, since all pieces of paper generate the same amount of heat, there have been no successes and, to date, three mid-air collisions.

Last year, a Tokyo firm used an experimental underground drilling rig to try to sneak into Mrs. Limpet's basement. The device, dubbed the Mole Machine, however, hit an underground electric line and all inside were electrocuted. "I couldn't watch my soaps for three days," she said. Other attempts have included sending midgets down the chimney and using cat psychics.

But the award for most ingenious has to go to New York's Sanhedrin Bros., which hired a German nanotechnology firm to design microscopic video-armed robots in the shape of fleas and drop them into the Limpet residence. The plan would have worked except for the fact that Mrs. Limpet gives Pepper a flea shampoo every week. "Every time she ran the tub," says one insider, "we lost 14 million dollars of robots."

The brokerages now face two problems because of Pepper. The first is that the

Webster's Message:

We're Dead, Wish You Were Here

Continued From First Page

have been flying that BTI is likely to close its doors in a paroxysm of liquidation, in a last-ditch attempt to draw even with Webster. Some workers will be given early retirement, while the rest will be made Vice Presidents, and then asked to kill themselves.

Industry analysts predict just such a move. "BTI is paying the price for its short-sighted, self-indulgent policy of continuing operations, while Webster is basking in glory," said Shiela Wardton, an analyst for Goldman, Sachs. "I'd look for BTI— and a lot of other companies, in a lot of other industries—to shrink into another dimension before the end of the year."

Officials from BTI were unavailable for comment. Most interpret this as only the first step in that company's attempt to use Webster's Zen strategy of non-existence.

MIT Prof Chomsky In, Left-Wingers Out at "New Look" Journal

NEW YORK—In a surprise move, the *Journal* today announced the hiring of Noam Chomsky, Institute Professor of Linguistics at the Massachusetts Institute of Technology, as the newspaper's new editor-in-chief.

In a news conference at the paper's headquarters in lower Manhattan, Professor Chomsky declared that he would reverse what he called the *Journal*'s "recent drift to the left, especially on the editorial pages."

Some *Journal* staffers had expressed surprise at Professor Chomsky's hiring due to their impressions of his political beliefs, but Chomsky said these impressions were mistaken, and the creation of "the liberal media." "I've been battling this my whole career," he fumed. "That's how they marginalize you."

Professor Chomsky's first act as editor was to hire "my great and good friend" Chilean general Auguste Pinochet as his deputy. Chomsky said his next moves would include the institution of whippings for indolent reporters and a series of editorials calling for an immediate nuclear strike against Cuba. "Sit back and watch the fireworks, folks," he said ebulliently.

The Death (and Resurrection) of a Salesman

By WAR O. T. WORLDS

"It is easier for a camel to pass through the eye of a needle than for a rich man to enter heaven," we are told in Matthew 5:16, and on the face of it, the statement seems straightforward enough. But this Biblical curveball doesn't mean what you think it does, according to a new book, *God's Salesman: Why Jesus Wants You to be a Commodities Broker.* T.L. Jargon, America's foremost theo-capitalist, writes that "softheaded misinterpretations of this wee little verse have sown troubles between Christ and God-fearing businessmen for two millennia. When I think of all the profitmaking opportunities that have been missed because of a simple Aramaic transposition, I weep. Listen well, and understand: Satan wants to keep you poor—and he will even screw with the Bible to do it."

According to Jargon, in Roman times, "the eye of a needle" was a colloquialism for the wide doorways of a temple. Moreover, camels were smaller then, rarely more than six inches high. Finally, and most importantly, by "pass through" Jesus actually meant "defecate upon." So a more accurate reading of this famous Biblical quote would be: it is easier for a little, tiny camel (akin to our modern raccoon) to defecate upon the steps of a temple, than it is for a rich man to enter Heaven. Even scholars are unsure what Jesus meant, and suggest that Matthew 5:16 is His idea of a joke. "Obviously, Jesus was out of his head, talking nonsense during this part. Any responsible Christian should disregard it, along with all that claptrap about 'thy neighbor's kine' and stoning the incontinent."

Exploding the myth of Jesus' antipathy towards profiteers is only the first of many unusual theories T.L. Jargon maintains in his new book. While in the publishing tradition of Og Mandino's *The Greatest Salesman in the World* and Peter Intestine's *You CAN Take It With You,* *God's Salesman* is the product of an ambition greater than either of these. It is the latest volume in Mr. Jargon's "E Pluribus Unum" series, which he started in 1962 after a series of head injuries. Others include *The Book of Job Says Get A Job!, Currency Speculation, Siddhartha-Style, Confucius Say: Buy Low, Sell High,* as well as the forthcoming *The Tao of Capitalism.* All are intended to demonstrate that, in Mr. Jargon's words, "The World's great religions are about one thing: getting rich, rich, rich!"

This thesis is a novel one, and has much going for it. Certainly, it is hard to understand why the loving God of the New Testament would judge the commercial sector of His flock so harshly. But as much as you desperately want to be convinced by Jargon's logic, his book is rendered a frustrating babble by factual mistakes and flights of fancy as outlandish as they are irresponsible.

God's Salesman opens with the traditional scene of Jesus' birth in the manger.

Bookshelf

"God's Salesman: Why Jesus Wants You to Be a Commodities Broker"
By T.L. Jargon

but in Mr. Jargon's version they are not there because there was no room at the inn. Instead, God—"the world's savviest stockpicker"—had advised Joseph to save his money and invest in Bethlehem Steel. Even here that the reader begins to notice a certain confusion on Mr. Jargon's part.

Next, he tells us, the wise men arrived with their gifts of gold, frankincense, and myrrh. The gold "the Baby Jesus decided to keep, as a hedge against Herod's inflationary monetary policy," but the other two He liquidated, using the proceeds to invest heavily in Judean real estate. "Before He was five days old!" Mr. Jargon writes, "Jesus had tripled his money! He wasn't called 'the Christ' for nothin'!"

Where was the Virgin Mary when this was going on? According to Mr. Jargon, out haggling with the contractors who were building the Son of God's own personal version of Graceland. "The actual layout of this magnificent home has been lost to time," *God's Salesman* informs us, "but we can speculate at will. Probably there was a heated indoor pool, or, if not, a hot tub. Bowling lanes in the basement, without question. We know He would have had a game room with a pool table—perhaps with a neon sign on the wall writing out 'King of the Jews' in multi-colored script.

New Bill Screams "Cultural Bankruptcy!"

By ROXANE OSCART

a shame born of his fabled humility.
The words "The United States of

Plus secret passages, and stairways to nowhere!"

The bulk of the book goes on in the same vein. Jargon asserts that Jesus was never a carpenter, but instead toiled in the vineyards of mutual fund management when he wasn't bankrolling several attempts to capture the America's Cup. Mary Magdelene wasn't a whore but a high-powered corporate lawyer "representing such heavy hitters as Shell, General Electric and Exxon." And it turns out that the famous "let he who is without sin cast the first stone" is a mistranslation. What Jesus actually said was "he who is without *debt*."

But the strangest part of this strange book is the end. When Pontius Pilate—"the Roman Empire's answer to the S.E.C."—sentences Jesus to death, Jesus tells the Apostles not to mourn, "for my father's kingdom is low-tax, high growth!" As He expires on the cross, however, He beseeches Heaven: "Oh God, why hast thou forsaken me—is my net worth too low?" Mr. Jargon then briskly wraps things up with an admonition to keep a diverse portfolio and avoid fluoridated water.

In short, the Jesus of *God's Salesman* is eerily like Ivan Boesky in sandals, Mike Milken with a full head of hair. Plus, he can set people on fire. Twisting the Gospels until they (and the reader) cry out in pain, Jargon long ago left valid historical interpretation behind and crossed into the Land of the Loons. Boys and girls, the book reviewer's lot is not an easy one. Sometimes I wish I could forget how to read.

Why Wait Until September? Place Your Gridiron Bets, Folks

By TERENCE MINDBENDER

Millions of dollars are spent every summer—and even more once the games begin—trying to predict which football teams will win, which will lose, and which won't cover the spread. So-called bellweather statistics like "yards-per-pass-attempt (ypa)," "field-position-differential (fpd)," and the perpetually overrated "final score (fs)" have been invoked for decades to make sense of the frightening maelstrom of sweat and commerce that is professional football.

The *real* crystal ball has, of course, been used for years by those in the know. The salmonella-ravaged 1953 season excepted, the "Scrabble City Father Multiplier" Method has perfectly predicted the coming league champion for the past *39 years.* Like reading the entrails of birds or planning a family based on testicular hardness, this method is foolproof.

How does it work? It's almost childishly simple: you start by giving each team the numerical value of its nickname as figured in Scrabble tiles. For instance:

Cowboys (15-4)= 3+1+4+3+1+4+1=17
Rams (7-9)= 1+1+2+1=5

The 49ers (11-6) are spelled out, which yields: 2+1+1+4+2+1+2+1+1+1=17. It's no surprise that the Cowboys and Niners are evenly-matched. "However," you may be asking, "doesn't this method favor teams with longer names?" No! If it did, the Scrabble-scoring method would be next to worthless, but it *actually tells a deeper story* than the won/lost records.

For instance, looking at won/lost records alone, the Tampa Bay Buccaneers (7-9) should be easy pickings for the Buffalo Bills (12-5). But the team names tell a different story: Tampa Bay scores a Dallas-like 17, while Buffalo tallies a very average 7. It's obvious to even the most casual fan that Tampa Bay is by far the better team—the final record for these two teams hardly reveals that the Buccaneers lost seven games after their players suddenly seemed unable to score touchdowns, almost as if they had been poisoned. The Bills, on the other hand, were accused by the "Phins Jimmy Johnson of running and passing with a staggeringly high, preternatural degree of accuracy; charges, which, to this writer, sound awfully close to witchcraft!

Okay, now comes the second stage: the City Father. The individual who founded the city where the franchise is located must be named and ranked according to appearances in *Who's Who,* available at your local library. For instance:

Houston (6-10): Sam Houston: 7
Seattle (7-9): Chief Achquinkgook: 9 (*Who's Who in Native America*)
Philadelphia (11-5): William Penn: 17

Now, of course, some will scoff and note that the Packers (11-5), are let down by the father of Green Bay, William Green, who pulls a miniscule 1. But that's where the multiplier comes into effect. Multiply Houston's 11 Scrabble points by their name value of 7 and you get 77. The same for Green Bay results in 16 x 1 = 16. Therefore, Houston, despite having untested players at all key positions, has a better chance at the title than the Packers, who have the league MVP, Brett Favre, at quarterback.

The Cleveland Browns-cum-Baltimore Ravens present a special case. While the Ravens would, under our SCF method, would normally rate a 54 (1+1+3+1+2+1=9, times 6 [Lord Baltimore, or Lord Raven, the record is not clear]), teams which move *and* change their names must start out at 0 for 3 seasons. Honest, it's always been like that.

Now for the money shot. Which teams are the leading candidates for post-season glory in 1998? Tampa Bay (SCF rating: 194) and Seattle: 164. Therefore, I predict Super Bowl XXXII will be won by Tampa Bay over the Seahawks, 33 to 21.

Some naysayers will claim that the weakness of this method is that the ratings never change from year to year, since the historical information and the team nickname never change. Therefore, Tampa Bay should win every year. The answer is, of course, most teams don't live up to their potential, or have key players injured, or just don't care.

So now you know what the big Vegas players know: the Scrabble City Father method is money in the bank. The NFL uses it to forecast Paul Tagliabue's travel plans for the playoffs; he's spent Christmas in Florida, by himself, for the last four years. The real Super Bowl isn't decided in January, but in the numbers, now and forever. That's the magic that is the National Football League.

seem to stay in business Lord knows how, and as you can imagine it all went down-hill from there...

New York

They say that every civilization gets the currency it deserves. According to legend, the ancient Assyrians, one of the most warlike peoples ever to inhabit the earth, used as their coinage huge stone tablets which could be smashed down on the heads of their opponents. It was said that the Assyrian army could rout an enemy with its spare change alone.

The Pharisees of Roman Jerusa-lem used gold pieces elaborately inscribed with a prayer emphasizing their preeminence among the Jews of the era. When the Romans wanted to round up the leaders of the populace, they simply held a "Pretty Money Contest." The vanity of the Pharisees, it is told, led them straight into the Roman prisons, torture, and death.

The Second Empire of Louis Napoleon III was a circus of ineptitude and pretension, embodied by the ridiculous *Grande Francs*, these measured 12 meters long and 3 wide, with a huge portrait of the Emperor on both sides. (At that size, however, it was possible to look up Napoleon's nose and see what is now known as a *booger*.) The Prussian Army, on its way to Paris in 1871, was delayed three days by having to navigate through piles of giant wallets, dropped in panic by routed French soldiers.

And now, in *fin de siècle* America, we finally have the money we deserve. In this age of "MTV-style" elegant violence, casual perversion, and apocalyptic terrors everywhere, we have the money with which future eco-historians will define decadent, delirious, us. We have the new one hundred dollar bill.

It is not enough that the numbers on the front of the note are so large they can be seen from space; they are arranged helter-skelter, as if by a toddler. The four 100's—the heart of the bill, if it has one—are rendered in eight separate styles. Andy Warhol has had his revenge. Benjamin Franklin's image is far larger than Washington, Lincoln and the others are on their respective currencies. Now I admire Mr. Franklin as much as the next man, but does the mild-mannered discoverer of electricity and patron saint of the Post Office really 4000% more important than George Washington or Grover Cleveland? Indeed, Franklin's countenance appears to be grimacing, as if from

America" are rendered so as to suggest psychedelia in its final throes. What is this, legal tender, or a poster for the Fillmore East? These letters would be better off on Ken Kesey's bus of Merry Pranksters, or at a Haight-Ashbury subversive bookstore, next to advertisements for naughty comics and hallucinogen-laced blotter paper (perhaps present-day bohemians will be caught licking the bills in search of some high; I, for one, can understand their mistake).

Flipping the note over brings no relief from the onslaught of bad taste. The staid, time-honored image of Independence Hall is framed by: nothing at all. The glaring white space practically explodes out of the bill, like some so-called "painting" by one of the abstract depressionists who have brought American art so low in the latter half of the twentieth century. With the horrors so visible on the rest of the money, I half expected to see that great building wrapped in nylon by Christo and his asinine ilk. Grrr!

The overall effect is of a hysteric laying out his case for the existence of UFOs before a captive audience, or of those blasphemous advertisement for McDonald's showing a group of nuns tap dancing in joy over yet another tasteless, cholesterol-laden meal. The juxtaposition of the images of a founding father and one of our most historic landmarks with the wacked-out, open-all-night lettering and color schemes may be some post-modernists' idea of a cultural statement. However, it strikes this reviewer as the most idiotic American note since the Confederate States of America's three-dollar bill (on which Jefferson Davis was shown serving a tray of mint juleps to Generals Lee and Jackson), or the U.S.A.'s first dollar bill, which simply had the words "Please accept this" superimposed over a rattlesnake cut into thirteen part.

Counterfeiting is not a laughing matter, and the Treasury is absolutely correct in trying to counter the attempts of nations like Iran and Nepal to destroy the American economy by circulating millions of fake c-notes. But if we are to sink to the level of cultural epilepsy in the design of our new currency, then America, it's sad to say, has already lost the day.

The Surgeon General Has Determined That This Parody is Very Funny.

CIGAR

Asphyxionado

WINSTON

WINSTON CHURCHILL: TINY PENIS?

THIRTEEN CIGARS TO AVOID

STOGIES OF THE GODS?

THE VIRGIN MARTINI

THE VIOLENT WORLD OF WORMFIGHTING

Coming Christmas 1997

From the folks that brought you THE BULL STREET JOURNAL. For more info or to reserve your copy, dial up www.titanicstudios.com or call (888) 727-6391. (What's that smell?)

Every Friday For the Next Four Years

Whitewater. Once conjuring scenes of wet, watery beauty, this innocent word has been stolen from us; now it is shorthand for the most depraved parade of acts in the history of mankind. Yea, "whitewater" only means one thing: evil.

In the years to come, we think it likely that a chastened humanity will use this word as part of the common tongue. "The pogroms were an act of purest *whitewater*." "To look into the eyes of Pol Pot was to know *whitewater*." "Hitler, Stalin, Mao: which one was the *whitewaterest*?"

Often our friends and relatives ask us to explain Whitewater, and we are always reluctant. How does one "explain" the Bataan Death March? But for our children's sake, and their children's, and their children's after them, and their children's children's' childrens's" (etc.), we must, in the following chronology, make the attempt. Also, note all the stuff you can buy from us.

September 8, 1947 Two-tailed "hairy" comet appears over Sichuan Province, China. Bantam fighting cock born to woman in Mexico City. A tornado of frogs buries twelve Texas towns. Hillary Rodham born in Chicago, Illinois.

1950 Hillary Rodham's mother enrolls her in a federally-funded daycare program, where she meets Sapphic playmates Lani Guinier and Anita Hill. Hillary Rodham will later write in *It Takes a Village Voice* that it was here she formed her lifelong allegiance to forced collectivization.

Call 1-800-123-4567 for our book
"No Makeup and Hairy Armpits"
The Bull Street Journal Guide to Hillary Rodham Clinton ($19.95)

1951 William Jefferson Clinton enters kindergarten in Hot Springs, Arkansas. On his first report card he receives a C in Handwriting and Spelling but an A+ in Shifty-Eyed Dissembling. On the comments section his teacher writes "Little Billy has an oily charm that will serve him well if he wishes to grow up to defraud the American public. Also, he's kissed all the girls in class, including me."

1953 Seven year-old Bill Clinton wriggles out of his obligation to serve in the Cub Scouts. In a letter to the troop leader he speaks of his "personal anguish" over his decision. Later, as his troop goes on dangerous camping trips, he organizes demonstrations against them.

1956 Vincent Foster, a sixth grader in S&L with shotguns. They use their booty to buy a tract of land in Whitewater, Arkansas, telling the zoning board they plan to use the land "either for resort homes, a casino, or mass graves for our political opponents."

1982 Clinton is elected Governor of Arkansas for the second time. His inaugural address becomes famous for its conclusion: "... so I stand before you tonight and make three pledges. First, that I will enrich myself through flagrant back scratching and conflicts of interest. Second, that I will boink dozens of bimbos, including Paula Jones and Gennifer Flowers. And third, that I will kill Vincent Foster." Not one word of this is ever to appear in the *New York Times* or the *Washington Post*.

Call 1-800-123-4567 for the board game
"The Liberal Media"
Ridicule Religion! Celebrate Deviance!
Amass wealth and power while deceiving normal Americans! That's the way to the top in... The Liberal Media! ($54.95)

1983-90 The Clintons' Whitewater venture steadily loses value. In a complex scam, Hillary invests in cattle futures, then orders 19 billion hamburgers for Chelsea's taxpayer-funded birthday party. Her investment rockets 3,200%.

1991 Clinton decides to run for president. In an effort to impress the national media with the progress made under his stewardship, he initiates Operation Potemkin State; it is a success, but necessitates the liquidation of 50,000 poor Arkansans. "Watch out," says a grinning Clinton at a news conference. "I'm crazier'n Saddam!"

1992 Clinton is elected president. Sharp-eyed reporters notice that Hillary travels everywhere with thirteen black cats and an incubus named Sean.

1993 In an inaugural interview with Ted Koppel, Clinton tells him that he's glad to be President, because "now I can finally kill Vince Foster." The First Lady rents an apartment in Georgetown under the name Clillary Rodham Hinton.

1994 Vince Foster found dead in Virginia park. The Secret Service searches everywhere for the President, finally finding him "practicing my golf swing" about to be picked up by a limosine for a midnight flight to Chicago. The First Lady appears as if from nowhere, smelling strongly of sulfur. Wendell Hubble, former partner of both Hillary and Foster, resigns from office, citing scurvy.

Bondservants of the Beltway

To go by the editorial pages uptown and nationwide, slavery in China has become a big issue lately. Not a huge issue, though—maybe even smaller than it should be. For the purposes of scale, let us assume that Chinese slavery is a smaller hulaballoo than the discovery of intelligent Life on Venus, but bigger than why yeast can't vote. Thus bracketed, there the issue sits, generating a lot of heat, but much less light.

One can't move more than a few feet in any direction in the Beltway circles I move in, without realizing that everyone who is anyone now owns someone. I.e., slaves. Has since the late '70's. A lot of them. And I have to say, this isn't the first time that this observer has noticed the slight whiff of hypocrisy eminating from the Potomac tidal basin.

It would be funny if it weren't so shameful: the idea that the very people stuffing their Georgetown townhouses or their McLean ranch estates to the rafters with human chattel, are decrying the Chinese or the Canadians for their similar practices. All this under the constant, sub-sonic whine of "human rights"—a term so nebulous as to mean almost *anything*.

Though it has been targeted for elimination under the bureaucracy-slimming provisions of the Contract with America, the huge-yet-shadowy Department of Human Registration maintains an up-to-date list of slaveowners. It's updated annually, and the list may surprise you. Of the 412 current congressmen who own slaves, only 202 are declared members of the Grand Only Party. The majority of masters are, in fact, liberal Democrats. It seems that a lust for rampant social tinkering doesn't include respect for freedom: independent representative Bernie Sanders of Vermont owned 39 himself, despite his socialist tendencies. Of course, this was second only to Sen. Ted Kennedy, who calls his 121 slaves "the Kennedy family legacy." For those playing at home, Kennedy's tally does not

Potomac Wretch

By Paul A. Googol

No, Luke—The Liberal Media is *Your* Father

By Elbridge Gerry

What must Bill Clinton and his minions be thinking as they survey the catastrophe they've created in the last four years? My guess is: *So what? We can always get our pals in ultra-liberal Hollywood to rewrite history for us.* But if you thought *Nixon* was bad, if you cringed at *JFK*, then you haven't looked lately at the mother of all cinematic revisionism: *Star Wars*.

Yes, the events depicted in the *Star Wars* trilogy took place a long time ago. Yes, they were in a galaxy far, far away. But that doesn't mean they don't have plenty to say about the politics of the here and now. And Hollywood's present crop of ideologues, from Streisand on down, likes nothing better than to shamelessly distort the history of our Universe to suit their Trotskyite agenda.

Lesson #1 is, don't expect the revisionists to get history right just because you wrote it down. As any honest student of the glory days of the Empire knows, the true hero of the times was Darth Vader, who was attempting to steer a moderate course between the admittedly conservative policies of the Emperor and the wild-eyed Jacobins of the Rebellion. Yet for its source material *Star Wars* totally ignores the volumes one and two of Lord Vader's autobiography—*Tears Behind the Mask* and *Songs the Emperor Taught Me*—and instead relies on a dubious mishmash of oral histories and reports from self-described "human rights" groups. Vader's memoirs make fascinating reading for anyone interested in the lonely life at the pinnacle of power, and are comparable in weightiness even to Henry Kissinger's *The Kissinger Years*; no executive can fail to identify with Vader's troubles with surly, incompetent underlings, or come away uninspired by his firm methods of dealing with such headaches. But of course an account like this is of no use to *Star Wars*' woolly-headed creators, since the effectiveness of their well-crafted propaganda would be destroyed by any contact with the hard truths of the real world. Self-indulgent adolescents can go gallivanting off to "rebel," but Vader had to deal with real problems, such as in his valiant struggles to bring to the Empire the stability necessary to attract crucial foreign investment.

Lesson #2: Don't expect filmmakers to care about getting even the most basic facts right. For instance, all contemporary observers record that Vader spoke not with James Earl Jones' rumble but in a high-pitched, girlish squeak. Moreover, the film gives no hint that Vader, a truly Gingrichian visionary, insisted that a fax machine be included in the control panel on his chest.

Mr. Vader

Lesson #3: Journalists and liberals in general are suckers for self-proclaimed "revolutionaries." From Che to Castro, from Princess Leia to Chairman Mao, they are effortlessly seduced by those who claim to represent the "little guy"; you might think such naïveté was laid to rest in the cold mass graves of Siberia, but think again. Take a closer look at the heroes of this radical epic:

- Luke Skywalker — a teen-aged malcontent with infantile ideas about "adventure"; oppressor of the proud nomadic Sand People
- Han Solo — smuggler, ne'er do well, admitted "scoundrel"; plays Danton to Skywalker's Robespierre
- Obi-Wan [sic!] Kenobi — wears quasi-Islamic robes, is master of the irrational and clearly anti-Western hocus-pocus he calls "The Force"
- Leia — "senator" from Alderaan, well-known hotbed of drug smuggling and galactic terrorism
- Yoda — a Brezhnev figure with a shaky grasp of standard syntax, quite possibly because well-meaning do-gooders never insisted that he learn mainstream English

The films, of course, regard this motley crew with unabashed awe, a point of view that leads to a blatant whitewashing of uncomfortable facts. For instance, the responsibility of the Empire for the Tatooin "atrocities" — the deaths of the Jawas and Skywalker's relatives — is presented as an open-and-shut case. But considerable scholarship now indicates that the Jawas died at their own hand, despondent at a lack of economic opportunity. Even more suggestive, the White Papers from the early Reagan Administration provide evidence that what murders did occur are attributable to time-traveling members of the FMLN.

The rape of the truth continues with the depiction of the so-called "Death Star." In five hours of film it is never referred to by its true name, "The Universal Co-Prosperity Sphere." No attempt is made to portray it as contemporary observers perceived it: a triumph of engineering and technology, a space-borne manifestation of the human spirit. If the Empire's attempts to win the hearts and minds of recalcitrant planets were more enthusiastic than absolutely necessary, they cannot be blamed in the face of the Rebellion's savagery.

Finally, and most revealing of all, there is the rosy depiction of the clearly Marxist communal society of the Ewoks. And they are presented as cute and lovable! About as lovable as the Khmer Rouge, I'd say. Here the true agenda of Lucas and his fellow travellers is unmasked: not justice, but a radical redistribution of wealth from the producers to the ungrateful rabble — the only possible outcome once you start down the primrose path of cultural relativism.

In conclusion, the moment has come for us to stand up to those who would pervert history. Just a brief stroll on today's campuses will show you how serious the effects of three decades of deceit have been: the slovenly values of the rebels are clearly ascendant, with no respect given to the traditional sobriety and good grooming of the Empire. It's time for the Empire to *really* strike back—it's time Bill Bennett and the Heritage Foundation stop writing editorials, and start making blockbusters!

Washington, Wigs and Oats

By Step. Hopkins

The 1996 Presidential election is past, but the laughter is just dying down. Every Depp bests Edwin Booth; *Hollywood Wives* is infinitely more entertaining than *Uncle Tom's Cabin*; I could go on.

could not have known this, but he paid homage to his powerful love of the Oat at nearly every meal until his death.

speaks of his "personal anguish" over his decision. Later, as his troop goes on dangerous camping trips, he organizes demonstrations against them.

1956 Vincent Foster, a sixth grader in Little Rock, Arkansas, is recruited by the Israeli Mossad. Training begins.

1968 Hillary Rodham graduates from Wellesley. Her senior thesis, "An All-Queer Military: Only a Matter of Time," is received warmly by a cabal of radical multiculturalist faculty. As later commentators will note, Wellesley students live in an estrogen-drenched, hothouse atmosphere at their all-woman college.

1969 Bill Clinton puffs on a "marijuana-joint" in front of seven credible witnesses, including a Supreme Court Justice and the Archbishop of Detroit. Soon thereafter he tells friends that loves to "get baked," and his speech becomes peppered with such anti-establishment phrases as "far out" and "groovy."

Call 1-800-123-4567 for the pamphlet *"President MaryJane, Our Pothead-in-Chief" by David Brock ($9.95)*

1970 Hillary Rodham meets Bill Clinton in the library at the Yale Law School. Fellow students recall that they would walk together for hours in rapt discussion of their common dream of stifling entrepreneurial initiative. Hillary excels in her courses, especially "Shady Real Estate Deals: From Conception to Coverup."

1973 Hillary Rodham and Bill Clinton are married in Little Rock. Hillary keeps her last name, because, she explains to friends, "it's more butch." At the wedding reception Clinton makes a pass at beauty queen Susan McDougal, promising that if she sleeps with him he will kill Vincent Foster.

1978 Bill Clinton elected Governor of Arkansas. On election night Hillary thanks her "coven" of female advisors for their "support and Wicca magik."

1979 Chelsea Clinton born. What a dog!

Call 1-800-123-4567 for the CD-ROM *"1,001 Cruel Jokes About the First Daughter"*
Order now and get Amy Carter supplement free!!! ($89.95 [specify Mac or Windows])

1980 Bill Clinton is defeated in a bid for reelection. He and Hillary, desperately short of funds, rob Madison Guaranty Lady appears as if from nowhere, smelling strongly of sulfur. Wendell Hubble, former partner of both Hillary and Foster, resigns from office, citing scurvy.

Call 1-800-123-4567 for the complete set of Whitewater dolls. Includes Jim and Susan McDougal, David Hale, Robert Fiske. Double-stuffed President doll is punchingly perfect. Leather-clad Hillary doll comes complete with stake, matches, and—just in case—a small silver bullet. ($49.95)

1995 The newly-Republican Congress reopens the Whitewater investigation. Al D'Amato asks the special prosecutor to focus especially on any Clinton connections with the Mafia; Jesse Helms calls Clinton an errand-boy for Philip Morris; Newt Gingrich accuses Clinton of being Speaker of the House. Meanwhile, Clinton asks the Library of Congress to research "the worst thing a President ever did." The First Lady's staff tells the press that she will be vacationing for the next two years on the astral plane.

1996 Jim Guy Tucker and both McDougals are convicted of fraud and sentenced to prison. The President states that he is "displeased" with the jurors' decision and obliterates each of their homes with a tactical nuclear warhead. "Believe me," an unshaven Clinton informs the nation in a marathon nineteen hour address, "if I'm going down, you're all coming with me. I've still got the Bomb, dammit."

Call 1-800-123-4567 for Whitewater t-shirts, foam hats, mugs, posters, towels, pens, jewelry, placemats, tablecloths, throw rugs, shoes, furniture, compilation albums, spears, etc. If we don't have it we'll make it.
Ask for price.

With the President's relection, the gruesome spectacle of Whitewater lurches on. Hannah Arendt wrote of "the banality of evil, and vice versa." Was she a foreigner? It doesn't matter, she was right as rain: serious times deserve serious measures. Far be it from us to suggest a coup d'état; all we can say is, Joint Chiefs, we know one editorial page you can count on. You might want to videotape them afterwards, like the Romanians did with the Ceauçescus, although if you throw some water on Hillary she may just melt.

Asides

Why not?

It's about time that we made the Senate hereditary.

course, this was second only to Sen. Ted Kennedy, who calls his 121 slaves "the Kennedy family legacy." For those playing at home, Kennedy's tally does not include his rotating army of indentured servants imported from the Auld Sod.

The slaving double-talk isn't limited to elected officials. Heads of such diverse NGOs like the ACLU, Human Rights Watch, the World Bank, and the National Symphony own slaves. So do the Secretary of State, the directors of the FBI, CIA, and NSA, and the owners of the Washington Redskins and Bullets. And the editors of the Washington *Post*, the Washington *Times*, and that beacon of liberal thought, *The New Republic*. (The Editor of the *National Review* does not indulge, claiming that they always "run away.")

Once upon a time, slavery may have been unfair to people of certain ethnic backgrounds, but just like poverty and dying, the practice cuts across many racial lines. Roughly 72% of today's slaves are white. Roughly 45% of today's slaveowners are white. Which means that roughly 27% of white people are slaves, and roughly 73% of Black and Hispanic Americans are white slaves. And vice versa. You don't need a degree in rocket science to see that this adds up to a national disgrace.

The real shame here is while ordinary Americans are denied their constitutional rights to own slaves due to meddlesome governmental interference, the bigwigs inside the Beltway are, as usual, helping themselves to the proverbial cookies from the proverbial cookie jar. It's nothing new: look at all the nuclear weapons owned by the government, while Tom Lunchpail and Sally Housecoat must make do with pitiful assault weapons and whatever nerve gasses are available at your local hardware store.

Why has this epidemic of homegrown slavery stayed out of the major news media? That's simple. The Washington offices of the New York *Times*, ABC News, and C-Span are filled with human property, doing light office work, making coffee, and troubleshooting the LAN. The highly-paid pundits who beat the drum of the nation's media membrane are unabashed offenders themselves; no wonder they're not rushing to shed some light on this travesty. Maybe Frank Rich (five slaves) and Anna Quindlen (three slaves and a consort) could find their way clear to turn their rhetorical guns on their own party's gross violation of the time-honored rule of "fair's fair"? I'm not holding my breath. Until then, we can expect that the slavery issue will stay out of the media's crosshairs.

Sadly, I am no longer surprised.

By Step. Hopkins

The 1996 Presidential election is past, but the laughter is just dying down. Every four years the bumbling American colossus bares its Achilles heel to a world whinnying with delight: the awesome inadequacies of its political candidates. Sadly, we have become so acclimatized to this sorry state of affairs that merely to mention that most of the people that run the country are not the types of folks you would let mow your lawn, is heretical. Let me speak plain: if our Presidential candidates were fish, we would certainly throw them back. If they were tomatoes, we would either grind them under our heel without a second thought, or give them to our children to throw at cars. We certainly wouldn't elect them to the highest office in the land!

And yet we elect these tomatoes, year after year after year.

What's wrong with our candidates—are they really worse now than ever before? Bearing the Burmese tiger trap of mythologizing in mind, it is painfully obvious that there *was* a time when political giants strode upon American turf, and now ain't it. If it appears unfair to compare Bill Clinton to Thomas Jefferson, that only underscores our unspoken conviction that the present President is a man of compromised competency. In every field of endeavor, modern Americans are improving upon their forebears—Michael Jordan is better than George Mikan ever was; so too Johnny Depp bests Edwin Booth; *Hollywood Wives* is infinitely more entertaining than *Uncle Tom's Cabin*; I could go on.

But not so our Presidential candidates. Comparing our present crop to even the acknowledged second rank of Chief Executives yields no balm for troubled minds. While it is common knowledge that Warren Harding spoke 17 languages (often in the same sentence, which left onlookers utterly flummoxed but impressed), during their debates, it was painfully obvious that neither incumbent Clinton nor challenger Dole could identify the World on a map. And while plain-speaking Harry S Truman was responsible for the complex mathematical calculations that led to the Atomic Bomb, checkbooks confiscated from both Dole and Clinton revealed that their accounts hadn't been balanced correctly in 7 years.

But how to change things? Using a popular study of Washington published in 1995, *Upon These Mighty Quadriceps...*, two keys to the Founding Father's greatness are evident: attire and nutrition. George Washington, like most men of his time, wore a wig. (And what's more, a powdered one.) This accoutrement undermined even Washington's fabled *gravitas*, causing more than one ragged Continental soldier to snigger, "Why should I listen to him? He wears a bleedin' wig." Thus, Washington had to compensate for his funny hair with wisdom and character. These proved strong enough to shatter the will of many a naysayer, and leave him quaking, incoherent.

Too often today's politicians are nothing more than empty suits. Some of these suits are very nice—but when choosing the Leader of the Free World, it is natural to want something more. It is clear that forcing Dole and Clinton to don freakish attire would have been good for them, and therapeutic for the rest of us. Only when they appeared wearing nothing but a powdered wig and wooden teeth, would these two consummate chameleons have been forced to reveal the man within.

Secondly, *Upon These Mighty Quadriceps...* makes a great deal out of Washington's diet, which consisted almost entirely of oatmeal. (Martha Custis often remarked that it was her oatmeal, not her irritating personality or uncertain grasp of personal hygiene, that kept their marriage strong.) This quirk is a perfect example of the first President's intuitive wisdom: modern studies have shown the once-scorned oat to be "the King of Grains," containing precisely the vitamins and minerals necessary for the founding of a new country. Washington could not have known this, but he paid homage to his powerful love of the Oat at nearly every meal until his death.

Let us contrast the dietary habits of Messrs. Clinton and Dole. The President's preference for greasy fast food is well-known. As an example of how this impacts upon his performance of the Presidency, not one bill that has passed his desk since 1993 has escaped without unsightly "special sauce" stains. And during the '96 campaign, Clinton was spied with McDonald's apple pies in his back pocket on no fewer than *ninety-seven* occasions.

But if Clinton was bad, the Kansan was worse. Few among us can honestly say we don't love a good hamburger, but the dietary territory staked out by Dole is quite disturbing. Peanut butter and mentholatum sandwiches? Paste? Live bugs? Even Dole's more pedestrian tastes give one pause: whatever one may think of his compulsion to on frozen hot dogs, it certainly doesn't give him the same nutritive punch as a bowl of steaming hot oatmeal, with or without raisins.

One thing is obvious: only after they are forced to wear silly old-timey duds and eat lots and LOTS of oats, will our Presidents be great again. Until we can repeat history, we are condemned to remember it—and remember, toohow painfully lackluster our Presidents truly are.

Step. Hopkins is Professor of Nincompoopery at Dartmouth.

Notable & Quotable

Now that the election's over, Bob Dole thinks it's time to tell the American people one of the most important things about Bob Dole: Bob Dole's a nudist. A big, moley, cover-Junior's-eyes-because he-might-have-nightmares nudist...See, Bob Dole learned in WWII that the Italians have a more relaxed attitude towards their bodies, a raw sexuality, which I never forgot, and always tried to emulate. Then years later, after I had entered politics, I learned my mentor and friend Dick Nixon was a nudist, and I was 'hooked'...Believe me, carrying this secret has been the most difficult thing Bob Dole's ever had to do. But I'm not the only one. There were twenty-seven other "nudies" in the Senate alone...Now, Timothy, would you hold my coat? You're all about to see where Bob Dole uses Coppertan's 'Xtra Strength for Pink Parts'...

—Bob Dole, speaking yesterday after being chosen "Coppertan's 1997 Man of the Year."

THE BULL STREET JOURNAL

Michael Gerber
Jonathan Schwarz
Robert Weisberg
Writers

Edited and Designed by
Michael Gerber

Todd Lynch, Cullum Rogers
Artists

Published by
BULL STREET, INC.
Editorial and Corporate Headquarters:
266 West Eleventh St., #2RE, NY, NY 10014
Telephone (888) 727-6391

Letters to the Editor

Packaging Should Be Seen, Not Obscene

I like a musical birthday card as much as the next guy, but I was nothing less than appalled at your article ["Giggling Guns, Singing Syringes...Even Condoms That Moan" Oct. 25] detailing the latest wave of audio chips in packaging. Your article glossed over Tops' new line of baseball cards, which have been banned in several states, outside of the South even. And with good reason—one of the tamer offerings has the mood-challenged Cleveland Indians outfielder Albert Belle screaming "Eat me!" whenever the card is exposed to light. Sure enough, these cards have piqued my seven year old's interest in the national pastime, but at the expense of teaching him the kind of florid, ready profanity I haven't heard since the Navy.

Perhaps through a misguided, pinheaded sense of even-handedness, Arthur Brainded's piece failed to strike a proper note of condemnation (much less outrage), opting instead for a whimsical survey on the growing phenomomon. If one can make a case for the Joe Camel cartoon luring underage smokers, certainly a little, squeaky voice exhorting them to "Breathe deep cuz ya get a bigger buzz!" is even worse. And Coors' new "Me Chief Chug-a-lug" jingle is not only extremely offensive to Native Americans, it irritated the hell out of me until after the sixth one.

RICHARD DIMWITTER
New York, NJ

Mr. Microsoft's Backend Architecchure

Call me old-fashioned, but I for one did not feel the need to read about Bill Gates displaying his anus to Microsoft's board of directors ("Gates Spreads 'Em," September 23). Perhaps I am showing my age, but I do not want to know when America's leading industrialist bends over, pulls apart the cheeks of his buttocks, and shouts "Take a look at my scuzzy port!" as stockholders and the press look on in shocked silence. In the olden days such lapses from public decorum were snickered about at the best clubs, not splashed across the pages of America's leading business newsjournal.

I am at loss to fathom what you believed your readers would gain from such coverage. Did you feel this would help us with our investment decisions? That our lives would be the richer for viewing your minutely detailed illustrations of the event? Have you, sirs, at long last lost your minds? Please cancel my subscription.

J. M. NICEFISH
Grosse Pointe, Mich.

As the manager of an investment portfolio and a witness to the event, let me be the first to commend the Journal on your splendid coverage of Bill Gates' impressive performance at Microsoft's annual board meeting. I only wish that you had had space to include Mr. Gates' comments about "our new product rollout" and "this sneak peak at Windows '96" during the climactic moment.

My sole quibble is with your description of onlookers as being "horrified and

The Laffer Curve Is No Laughing Matter

I was heartened to read Scrimshaw Shinbone's impassioned defense of the Laffer Curve and the trickledown theory for which it stands. At least one professor refuses to the hew to the line of wishywashy economic egalitarianism that infects America's academies like kissing disease.

To me and my friends, personal wealth is like a delicious dessert. Up to a certain amount, it is devoured with singleminded relish; however, after one is full, consuming even one mouthful more is distasteful in the extreme. Pleasure's border has been silently crossed, and one finds oneself trapped in the land of Torture! At this point, who would not say to one's tablemate,

Letter From the Publisher

To Our Readers:

A publication, any publication, is like a Frankenstein's monster: it is the living, breathing product of the labors of many expertly-trained professionals, each with only a limited knowledge of what they are doing, and why. Some would say it also flies in the face of God.

Anyway, after a frenzied period of creation, each issue snaps its restraints like so many twigs and storms out of our ancestral Castle, to enlighten or wreak havoc, depending. If our monster, *The Bull Street Journal*, has caused any trouble over the previous year, we wholeheartedly apologize. (*Hint:* look for missing girls in the town well.) In our defense, we can only say that thanks to our inept assistant Igor, we put an abnormal brain in the editorial page by mistake. As soon as we recapture it, we'll put a good one in, we promise. Maybe Jimmy Carter's, if he's not using it.

A readership, on the other hand, is like a family, with the publication acting as *paterfamilias*. But remember what a publication is like. (See above.) Now perhaps you see how dangerous a free press can be. If Frankenstein/Dad—the *Journal*, please try to keep up—went berserk and tried to strangle you or injure you in any other way, financially-speaking, we are sorry. We really did believe that there was going to be a worldwide shortage of sand in the first quarter. We're still scratching our heads.

Nevertheless, it has been a profitable year for *The Bull Street Journal*. Oh, very profitable indeed. We trust it was also profitable for you, our readers, too. We also trust that you are glad for us, that it was as profitable for us, as it was profitable for you. If in fact it was profitable. For you, we mean. It was very profitable for us, anyway, and like to think that what's profitable for us is profitable for you, too. Pardon us— we're a little confused. We trust you, our readers, are, too. Also.

Our time-honored philosophy, which can be summed up and even put to music as "Free people, free markets, free martinis from 4 to 6" continues to be wildly time-honored with advertisers and corporate public relations departments alike. All of you, our readers, ought to try this philosophy some time. Even if no ads get bought, there's a lot of gin, vermouth and vodka hanging around the office, which makes creating this monster one Hell of a lot less painful. I can't even feel my fingers right now, that's how less painful it is. You can't get much less painful than that. Without dying.

Where was I? Who knows? Looks like a bunch of chicken-scratches.

Looking over a few issues forced into the window jamb to keep the wind out, I notice there were a lot of stories in the *Journal* this last year. Every page is full of them! Who would have thought that we could have written so many things? I am particularly proud that we printed

nothing about the O.J. Simmons trial, spurning the sensationalism that ran amok around us. While our competitors reveled in the tasteless and tawdry insand-outs of a gruesome celebrity murder, the *Journal* refrained from appealing to our readers' baser instincts, and concentrated on uncovering ways for them to make buckets of money. Ah, money— according to our computer, we mentioned 17 quintillion dollars last year, more than any other publication. This figure represents an increase of 15% from the same period in 1995 and is light-years from our historical low, a buck-fifty, posted in 1957-8. Why do we go to the trouble to reveal actual dollar amounts in our articles, unseemly as it may seem? Because you, our readers, want us to.

We have become fully computerized in the last year, which has allowed us to do the entire issue on computer. Also, too, it enables us to keep strict control on all the staff's punctuative activities, and we have slowed the petty theft of commas, decimal points, and other office supplies—at epidemic proportions only six months before, and threatening the company—to a minimum. This has allowed us to cut our costs by roughly $2,000, which we have invested in better news coverage, staff hats, et cetera.

the *Journal*, including one for dead birds. We hope that the next year will bring each one of these extremely expensive freestanding publications a highly-targeted audience. Or any audience. Say, five each to start. Buy a copy, help us out.

But I would be remiss if I did not state some of the times that the *Journal* failed to live up to its impossibly high—nay, Godlike—standards. Of course, there was the aforementioned sand-shortage scare we led in February. And there was our ill-advised editorials (suggestions, really) that readers boycott the income tax. We never dreamed that so many people wouldn't get the joke. Finally, there was our insistence that readers should pull their money out of the stock market, and invest it in questionable orgone-based cancer cures. You can rest, assured that the halls of our offices ran red with the blood of the staffers responsible for each one of these snafus, and that we will do our best to do our best to do better in 1997 and beyond.

This letter continues a tradition two decades long, and reflects our belief that publishing a newspaper is a public trust, somewhat like running a State Park. As such we ask you to leave the paper in as good a condition as you found it, and not doodle in the margins. For in the end we are accountable to you, our readers—our "family." Not so accountable, however, that you can just barge into our offices whenever you want. Remember, we're a monster; we'll throw you out—or worse!

Speaking of computers, *The Bull Street Journal* is aggressively pursuing electric publishing. The previous year has seen the launch of no less than 413 sub-editions of

Dear Mr. President:

For the sake of future generations, common decency demands that you act NOW.

"Injustice anywhere is a threat to justice everywhere."
Robert Fitzgerald Kennedy
Martyred the Fourth of June, Nineteen Hundred and Sixty-Eight

We, the undersigned, come from many countries, from many religious traditions, from many professions, from

would not say to one's tablemate, "Here—take mine—I'm stuffed"? It is only self-interest.

Ask yourself: have you ever heard a very rich person say anything good about money? No! The rich, more than anyone else, know the dangers of excessive wealth—and the exquisite thrill of slipping some extra zabaglione to the deserving mendicant.

It's a sorry thing to see the Socialists in Democratic clothing constantly vomit all over the memory of the great Andrew Mellon and his ideas. Thanks, Shinbone, for the chance to turn the spew in the other direction!

ERSKINE COCCYX
Princeton, New Jersey

Getting a Piece of the Pie

I love pie, don't you? Cherry pie, blueberry pie, even the much-maligned mince pie. Yumm. There's nothing like a warm pie, just taken out of the oven, steaming hot. Or, conversely, a pie that has been hidden in the back of your freezer for months and is now hard enough to hammer nails with. Sometimes pies are gentle and comforting, like a soft flannel nightgown and hot camomile tea; sometimes pies are brutal and cruel, like basketball-sized fragmentation grenades. Sometimes, at the very best times, they are both at once.

Where am I going with this? Who cares? The point is, vote Republican in '2000.

HAROLD YES-YES
Chicago, Ill.

---

tion of onlookers as being "horrified and sickened." While there were brief seconds of confusion, most present were delighted by the boldness of his action and not a few gave him a standing ovation.

Moreover, far from being an aberration, it is well known that such behavior is common among America's chief executives and is merely a way of displaying their "plumage," much as the strutting male peacock will fan his magnificent tailfeathers. I well remember the day the entire senior management of GM proudly exposed their "rosebuds" to an auditorium full of institutional stockholders in 1985; that day GM stock rose 89%, borne aloft on a wave of investor confidence. Who knows? Perhaps if Steve Jobs had had the initiative to display his famous a——e to a marveling world he would still be at Apple today, instead of languishing at Pixar. Please renew my subscription, now and forever!

ARNOLD SNIP
New York

Scissors, Snot and Sufferage

As one of the most ill-informed and apathetic citizens of the United States, I rarely write letters to your fine newspaper. But something startled me out of my usual sloth-like indolence yesterday, and I felt I should share some my misguided, cretinous ideas with your readers. These ideas are: (1) "Mowing" lawns with scissors; (2) The national beverage? Snot! (3) Sufferage for chickens How about it?

ROBERT MERMAN
California, California

Salt 'n' Pepa

One Woman's Opinion
Put out to Tory pasture, I see
When Elizabeth goes R.I.P.
The obvious choice to reign is Me.
Hanging out in NYC
Airing dirty laundry on TV.
Fragments of the Royal Family

Willie's a minor,
And Minor's a wimp,
Fergie's a trollop,
And Charles, a chimp.
The world's fed up
with their asinine frolics—
Bring in "Queen Ironn"* to the rest,
I say, "BOLLOCKS!"
M. Thatcher

Daffynitions:
Labor unions: a mob of good-for-nothing Red anarchists.

"Don't worry, honey— it's just the 'Invisible Hand'!"

We, the undersigned, come from many countries, from many religious traditions, from many professions, from many experiences, and hold beliefs as varying as the great spectrum of Humanity. But we all agree on one thing:
IT'S TIME TO ACT

"When they came for the gypsies, I did not speak up because I was not a gypsy. When they came for the homosexuals, I did not speak up because I was not a homosexual. When they came for the Jews, I did not speak up because I was not a Jew. And then, when they came for me, there was no one left to speak for me."
Deitrich Bonhoffer
Martyred the Fifteenth of March, Nineteen Hundred and Forty-Four

For too long now the world has been shamefully silent, has stood by in tacit approval, has chosen not to see. We come together now to say:
NO LONGER

"He who passively accepts evil is as much involved in it as he who helps to perpetuate it."
Martin Luther King, Jr.
Martyred the Fourth of April, Nineteen Hundred and Sixty-Eight

No longer will we turn our eyes away. No longer will we be deaf to the cries of children. No longer will we, the comfortable, harden our hearts and ignore this,
THE GREATEST INJUSTICE OF OUR TIME

"Some men see the world as it is, and ask why. I see what could be, and ask, why not?"
Robert Fitzgerald Kennedy
Martyred the Fourth of June, Nineteen Hundred and Sixty-Eight

For all people of good conscience there is a moment in their lives unlike any other, a moment when they must stand and be counted. History demands no less. For us, the undersigned,
THAT MOMENT IS NOW

"If not us, who? If not now, when?"
Person Who Said This
Whatever Date He/She Was Martyred

We therefore ask of you what we have asked of ourselves. It is all too easy to simply turn the page and forget. But we beg you to do whatever is necessary, whatever must be done, because
IT MUST STOP

"Some believe that the actions of one person can make no difference. But I believe that the ripples created by the actions of individuals can join together in a mighty wave and sweep down the highest walls of tyranny."
Robert Fitzgerald Kennedy
Martyred the Fourth of June, Nineteen Hundred and Sixty-Eight

So we join our voices in chorus and speak in one voice:
IN HOPE, NOT FEAR
IN LOVE, NOT ANGER
IN PEACE, NOT WAR

"It is better to light a single candle, than to curse the darkness, for their light can warm the World."
Adlai Stevenson
Martyred the Seventh of July, Nineteen Hundred and Sixty-Five

Susan Sontag
Salman Rushdie
Martin Amis
Kurt Vonnegut
E.L. Doctorow
Marian Wright Edelman
Sting
Bishop Desmond Tutu
Abu Jamal Mumia
Nelson Mandela
His Holiness the Dalai Lama
Vaclav Havel
Camille Paglia
Susan Sarandon
Reinhold Niebuhr
Hillary Rodham Clinton
Alice Walker
Gloria Steinem
Toni Morrison

Robert Fitzgerald Kennedy
Yoko Ono
Timothy Leary
The LA Clippers
Dr. William Cosby, Ph.D.
Jesse Jackson
Eugene McCarthy
Voltaire
George McGovern
Alexander Cockburn
Walter Mondale
Rev. Ralph Abernathy
David Geffen
Michael Lerner
Victor Navasky
Maharishi Mahesh Yogi
Nat Hentoff
Murray Kempton
Norman Mailer
Mikhail Bakunin

Coretta Scott King
Daniel Patrick Moynihan
Alec Baldwin
Elie Wiesel
Steven Spielberg
Cornel West
Jerry Brown
Paul Newman
The Emperor of Japan
Robert Redford
Oliver North
Andrew Young
Ann Richards
Richard Gere
Jimmy Carter
Norman Lear
Linda Bloodworth-Thomson
Peter Gabriel
Bill Bradley
Ralph Nader
The artist formerly known as Prince
and
Strom Thurmond

POLITICS AND POLICY

CIA Denies Everything

By FRANS. LEWIS

Staff Reporter of THE BULL STREET JOURNAL.

LANGLEY, VA—After weeks of pressure from groups as varied as the Black Congressional Caucus and VH1, CIA Director John Deutsch announced today, "after an extensive search of our files, we have found that all materials related to Project Pablum—uh, *so-called* Project Pablum—have been systematically removed and destroyed. Or, never existed." Shifty-eyed and nervous, Deutsch left, then remounted the podium and declared. "Everything on 'The X-Files' is true!" The Director then ran out of the room; his whereabouts are unknown.

Mr. Deutsch's less-than-reassuring performance was more grist for a mill of conspiracy that has been turning ever-faster following a six-part series in the *San Pachinko Intelligencer-Bee*. The series' thesis—long discussed as fact on black talk radio—is that career criminals, with the aid of the CIA, have been forcibly selling recordings of New Age synth-noodler John Tesh in America's ghettoes since the early 1980's.

One of this theory's most vocal proponents is Maxine Waters (D-CA). "I have nothing against Mr. Tesh," she recently said, "but we're talking holocaust."

As other papers have picked up the story, the *Intelligencer-Bee's* reporting has come under attack. But Hawley Smoot, the paper's "Editor," is unapologetic. "Facts?" What good are your 'facts,' in a world gone mad?"

Still, there seems to be at least some historical foundation for the argument. In his seminal 1987 book, *The Director Wore A Dress*, author Ferdinand Bull writes that for the last few decades of his life, J. Edgar Hoover was obsessed by what he called "race music." The Director often appeared at concerts incognito, dressed to look like—in his eyes, at least—a heavily made up black woman called "Charmayne." As was so often the case, Hoover's private obsession soon became public-policy. "Their music is *so* much better than ours," he groused in a 1965 memo. "And Clyde [Tolson] thinks that Sam Cooke is just *too* pretty." FBI agents were regularly dispatched to

Beasts of Burden Now Burdens On Society

Legal Snafu Highlights Rampant Illiteracy Among Farm Animals

By BUTTON GWINNETT

Button Reporter of THE BULL STREET JOURNAL

HAYWARD, WI — "We'd give the cows the W-2 forms, and when they couldn't fill 'em out, they'd start to cry," said Harry Ross, a lifelong dairy farmer, who has seen his herd plummet from 6,500 cows to just over ten in the last year. "You ever seen a cow cry? It's a damn pitiful sight.

"Since they couldn't fill out their forms, we had to let them go. I see some of 'em in town once in a while, lookin' rough, buying cheap wine and lottery tickets. I guess they're on the Welfare now."

This is the human—and bovine—side of the Bench Bill, which took effect in late 1993. Since then, it has had a disastrous effect on the dairy, honey, and caviar industries, among others. Hardly Draconian on the face of it, the legislation aims to cut down on the number of small employers employing various ploys to underreport the number of employees they, er, employ.

No one is questioning the guidelines' original intent; but thanks to this sloppily-written legislation, dairy farmers must fill out a W-2 Form for each one of their cows—which the cows then have to read, demonstrate comprehension of, and sign. Bovine literacy in the United States is just 0.2%, the lowest of any industrialized nation, roughly equal to that of Bangladesh. Statistics are grimmer still for chickens, and the Department of Agriculture has estimated that fewer than 30 of the nation's 50 billion bees—0.00000006%—can read and write. No statistics are available for fish, but experts doubt that any can write, though some may be able to read.

Under the Bench bill, chickens qualify as independent contractors "selling" their eggs to the farmer in return for bed and board. This injection of free market principles into a win-win relationship that has stayed essentially unchanged for at least 5,000 years, has had devastating effects across the board. Milk production, a reliable indicator of cow activity, is down 25% from last year, at its lowest levels since the late 1960's, when a emerging bovine Marxist movement, answering

at the point of a pistol, being forced to have sex with a bull."

"It's getting ugly out there," said Lester Young, a sheriff in Nebraska's famed Caviar Belt. "Every Saturday night, another gas station is knocked over by a school of liquored-up sturgeon. It's bad, but it'd be worse if they weren't so easy to catch." Police suggest that massive numbers of barnyard crimes go reported, because most of the perpetrators are eaten soon after being apprehended.

Still, some observers remain upbeat about the Bench Bill. "There will be an unavoidable period of dislocation as the market adjusts," said Joseph Schmitt, head of the Lexington and Concord Group, an economic think-tank based in San Jose. "Once cows, bees, fish, chickens and the like are educated, we believe that they will then be able to auction their bodily products to the highest bidder, and presumably increase their standard of living. Previously, their economic security was paid for by a low standard of living. This is reminiscent of the situation in the USSR. Haven't you ever read *Animal Farm*?"

The Bench bill was not always so controversial—it whisked through both houses in a record six and a half minutes, thanks to strong bipartisan support. And even now, as discontent grows, both parties continue to support it, "it has something for everyone," explains Rob Dentyne, a political consultant in Washington. "Think about it: the Republicans love the free-market, let's get the government out of our yoghurt angle, even if it means throwing millions of cows on the street. And the Democrats know that teaching all those animals to read and write will take a huge number of government jobs; which they could then give out of it. Hmmm... if such comes to

'No Politicians Necessary'

HUGE *Pile of Money Launches Third Party Bid*

By THO M°KEAN

Stiff Reporter of THE BULL STREET JOURNAL

WASHINGTON—With the actual election still years away, the 2000 Presidential race may be over before it begins: all of the money in America has finally announced its candidacy for the highest office in the land. "After a lot of soul-searching, I decided it was time to cut out the middleman," said the money, $93 billion worth, speaking in front of the Treasury Department this morning. "Al Gore and Jack Kemp are good men—I know them both well. But they take time out to eat and sleep. I, as the physical manifestation of a nebulous concept, need do neither; Plus, I'm cute as a button."

Not yet decided on a running mate, Money said that it is leaning towards either Corporate America, or the GNP.

Reaction to the news was swift. Money's candidacy was immediately endorsed by Steve Forbes, Alan Greenspan, Paul Volcker and, via ouija board, Alexander Hamilton. President Clinton appeared surprised when informed at a news conference; during his subsequent ninety-four minute discussion of the subject most reporters present lost consciousness.

Pundits agree that Money's candidacy creates the largest headaches for the Republicans, who had been wooing it to join the '00 ticket with retired General Colin Powell as Vice President. The Pro $$$ faction, led by the late Nelson Rockefeller, announced that it now favors running either "an expensive painting or a jewel-encrusted tiara." But Ralph Reed, leader of the Christian Coalition, said this alternative was unacceptable and that his followers planned to start a party of their own to run either Pat Buchanan, Bo Gritz, or—"under a best case scenario"—Jesus Christ.

In a reaction to Reed's announcement, Carl Sagan, chairman (posthumous) of the Unapologetic Atheists Party, announced that their '00 candidate would be "the Scientific Method." RossPerot announced that his candidate was still Ross Perot.

The big question is this: can Money win? "On the plus side, it's already got 100% name recognition," said William Schneider of the American Enterprise Institute. "On

France has cast a majority of its Presidential ballots for "Cheese." Moreover, Money can claim an impressive political pedigree: its great-grandfather, Wealth, almost captured the Republican nomination in 1892, and its granduncle, Das Kapital, was a player in Bismarck's Germany.

Certainly Money seemed the one to beat on the Treasury steps this morning, as it delivered a ringing denunciation of politics as usual. Speaking in a high-pitched, squeaky voice, it pledged that if elected it would establish a "Novus Ordo Seclorum." Money added. "I can't be assassinated, because I'm fungible!"

Even Washington's hardest-nosed reporters were charmed as Money parried questions with wit and aplomb; asked if it favors the death penalty, it grinned and replied, "Only for credit cards." Money even warned the journalists not to lose their objectivity, and fall in love with it: "Remember, that's the root of all evil."

As a further sign that Money is for real, Beltway insiders point to the appointment of political operative Roger Ailes as campaign chairman. (Ailes was rumored to have taken—irony of ironies—a large pay cut to come onboard.) "I think we're going all the way," says Ailes. "Of course, it's different than working for a regular candidate. I can't call it on the phone—I have to go to an ATM. And I wear rubber gloves so my hands don't get dirty when I touch it." Ailes laughs, his stomach shaking like a bowl full of jelly. "Course, I did that with Dick Nixon, too!"

Little is known about Money's personal life. A lifelong bachelor, friends say it has been burned in the past by women who were only after it for itself. Recently, Money has been linked to Pamela Harriman, doyenne of the Washington social scene and current ambassador to France, although paparazzi have recently spotted her with the Yen.

In any case, with Decision '00 only forty-six months away, the adrenaline in the campaign at Money's national headquarters. Campaign volunteers wear the smiles of those who believe they just might be working for the next President. Energized and confi-

Harry Ross

agents were regularly dispatched to record stores, with instructions to scratch Motown records. Twenty years later, or so the story goes, Project Pablum was born.

In the meantime, other "CIA-culture-blanding" theories are popping up like mushrooms, each ranging from unassailable to unlikely to the stuff that 'zines are made of. According to a forthcoming book, *The Lighter Side of the CIA*, recently declassified documents reveal that Jerry Lewis was purposely introduced into France to destabilize DeGaulle's government. On the other side of the spectrum, a New York-based citizen's group holds that comedian Harvey Korman's inexplicable popularity "bears all the fingerprints of the American intelligence community."

In this context, the lantern-jawed, sparsely blond, possibly computer-generated Tesh seems small potatoes, or at least business as usual. According to Mario Cuomo, the underachieving conscience of the Democratic Party: "John Tesh on any terms is bad enough, but to find out your own government is behind it...I'd say I'm shocked, but nothing shocks me anymore."

'Asphalt Is A Harsh Mistress, Man'

Continued From First Page

the chin and lower lip], I'd vote for him," said Horshack, a peripatetic barista. "If he got tatted [tattooed], I'd vote for him...He's pierced? Ahh, the nipple is *nothing*." Both were unaware that the election was long since over, and that they could not vote for the President, pierced nipple or no. It seemed mean to tell them so we didn't.

The President's opponents on the right slammed him for trying to "turn politics into some sort of mutant decathalon." An already defensive Jack Kemp declared defiantly, "I will not bungee jump in 2000—because of my knees." Kemp did not respond to this reporter's queries as to the state of his nipples.

Pat Buchanan, fresh from a GOP-arranged vacation tour of Greenland, Iceland and the Aleutians, crowed loudly over the President's accident. In a speech to the Federation of Xenophobic Lunkheads, he noted the "delicious irony" of the pro-NAFTA, pro-GATT President hitting a foreign car. "If he'd been doing his job, maybe that car would've been in a parking lot in Osaka, where it belongs."

At this point, everyone in the audience barked like dogs.

since the late 1960's, when a emerging bovine Marxist movement—unquestionably a fashion of the times—torpedoed milk production. (Luckily, the Red Holsteins were quashed by the FBI before impacting the American pocketbook.)

Production of eggs, caviar and honey are similarly down, despite lucrative incentive packages being offered to those animal Einsteins that remain legal. With so many out of work, it isn't surprising that many rural towns are reporting skyrocketing levels of crimes perpetrated by animals. "You live with them all your life, you think you know them," said Ross, "and then some night you find yourself eating

disputes of people, and leave the animals out of it...However, if push comes to shove, I wouldn't rule out the possibility of hiring pets as strikebreakers."

As public anger has mounted, the government has closed ranks, trying to focus the debate on the bill's original intention, and avoid addressing its bizarre side-effects. In an effort to mollify a surly citizenry, White House spokesman Mike McCurry said, "Think about your local copy shop. Sure, there are a few pimply creeps behind the counter, who are on the books. But then there's the guy who collates and staples, the troglodyte who picks the scraps off the floor, the drooling burnout who sits around eating

ernment jobs; which they could then give to their shady political cronies or unqualified minorities, or both."

of the American Enterprise Institute. "On the minus side, it's not a person—as much as we wish it were." But how large a problem is this? After all, twice in this century

the next President. Energized and confident, they toil beneath a banner emblazoned with their venture's motto: "Vote Money in '00: It's the Nation's Capital."

THE BULL STREET JOURNAL

MARKETPLACE

TECHNOLOGY AND FAMILY
By Sonny Sanjose

Overworked Parents Get With the (Computer) Program

For the family which has everything but quality care for their children, technology once again comes to the rescue. An ingenious computer program can take care of the children while mommy and daddy take care of business. VirtualParent 1.0 (Windows 3.11, Windows95, Macintosh, $99.99) takes the place of expensive child care centers, illegal alien nannies, and insane female au pairs with knives. It can play, explain cartoons, read, prepare meals, and even talk baby talk. The software is a godsend for many parents who have had to rely on brief windows of "quality time" in order to watch their children grow up, leave home, and hate their parents.

"I had always thought computers were only good for games," says VP user Lyle Barnadow. "But VirtualParent is even better than tv, because it really interacts with the children. At least, that's what the box says. I don't understand computers. I don't understand children either." VirtualParent has gathered raves from such diverse sources as *Parenting* magazine ("VP frees up parents from spending time with parents so that they can concentrate on becoming better parents — four disk drives!"), and *PC World* ("VP frees up computers from spending time with parents so that they can concentrate on becoming better computers — four disk drives!"). Perhaps inauspiciously, the most posi-

tive we go or else he starts screaming," says Cordelia Lear. Wylie Yammerand claims that the computer imprinted itself on his daughter, so that she asks to be shut down

every night instead of being put to bed. He is suing BioDyne for $1 billion and a new daughter. [The case has since been settled, with Mr. Yammerand receiving $1,000,000 and sharing the custody of a newborn baby girl with BioDyne.]

Also keeping BioDyne's tech support people busy is the fact that most of the code-writing for VirtualParent is done in India by programmers with an dubious command of the English language. This writer has heard the computer tell three young children at bedtime that "It is the sleeping, and sleeping will bed the sleeping" and "lie down in the sandwich or eat nails" at meals. According to Poon, the phrases are Sanskrit idioms which do not translate cleanly and insists that BioDyne has no plans to change the way VirtualParent is programmed. "English is a pretty weird language too. 'Take a chill pill'? What the hell does that mean?"

Once-Booming Cadaver Market Now "Worse Than Dead"
Corpses, Renewable Resource, Provide Everything From Eyedrops to Ersatz Pastrami

By PORTLAND OREGON
Staff Reporter of THE BULL STREET JOURNAL

Seemingly risen from the grave, tiny Orchid Bluffs, Montana, seethed with economic activity just twelve months ago. But today, this desolate, wind-raked burg

GRAVEROBBIN'

once again looks like a ghost town, and the dreams of yesterday bear the foul stench of decomposing expectations.

Some residents believe they've been cursed: "It's our fault for trafficking in Abominations," says Tom Quetzalcoatl, manager of Orchid Bluffs' lone restaurant, a Dairy Queen quietly going to seed in the center of the city. But others see not the vengeful hand of God, but the invisible hand of the market, curled tightly around the town's throat. Foolishly, Orchid Bluffs rode a single industry until it went bust: the business of dead human bodies. But while the industry itself may be shocking, the town's losing gamble is all too familiar.

My Taut Buttocks

It started three years ago when Belgian action star Jean-Claude Van Damme was filming his directorial debut. *My Taut Buttocks*, in nearby Birch Hills. For the climactic scene ("A grotesque orgy of beautiful violence" according to Roger Ebert) the film's producers wanted to use real corpses for verisimilitude's sake. Bells went off in the head of longtime Orchid Bluffs resident, ex-high school Econ teacher Marvin Grimoire.

"I figured, if there's anything Orchid Bluffs has, it's dead people," says Grimoire. Indeed. The town sits on top of an abandoned plutonium mine and is directly downwind of a nerve gas factory with a history of egregious safety viola-

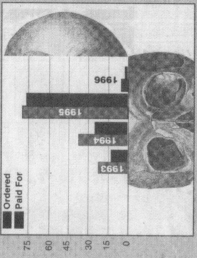

The Life and Death of Well...Death

Number of dead bodies produced by
Orchid Bluffs, Montana in thousands

- Ordered
- Paid For

1993
1994
1995
1996

0 15 30 45 60 75

Source: Channelhouse and Garden

tion on the social fabric of Orchid Bluffs. "Remember when you were eight, and your sister sat on 'your side' of the car seat?" explains social worker Marge Oleo. "You wanted to kill her, right? Well, what if you could have made $65,000 by doing it?"

Not surprisingly, the average number of children per family dropped swiftly from 3.4 to exactly one. And it wasn't long before the adults got in on the act, slaughtering countless friends and coworkers. The once-quiet Orchid Bluffs nights were now a cacophony of shotgun blasts, chopping hatchets, and anguished screams.

"Still," says Grimoire, "our per capita income went through the roof! I think this is a perfect example of what Joseph

deal looked heaven sent. "Let's face it, we make Bangladesh look like a mineral spa," explains Grimoire, "but as the economist David Ricardo would put it, that's exactly our comparative advantage!" So with the entrepreneurial spirit that made this country great, Grimoire went from door to door, offering his friends and neighbors $20 for every freshly-dead loved one.

There's Gold in Them Thar Holes

Soon his firm, named Charon Partners, was a blaze of economic activity, as he ordered business cards and an "Out to Lunch—Back in Five Minutes" sign. As it turned out, Orchid Bluffs and its new industry of "chattlery" was perfectly positioned to catch a cresting wave. Not

and knives and crazies.

Body prices started to drop, and criticism began to mount. The National Council of Churches, in a widely publicized statement, called the industry "the grossest thing ever." Grimoire, by this time president of the National Association of Chatteliers, was unrepentant: "Frankly, the desecration of corpses just makes good business sense. I think being freed from the bonds of all human morality is exactly what America needs."

More serious, though, was the competitive threat from big conglomerates, led by Germany's I.G. Farben. Then there was the expansion of supply from abroad, as the World Bank began requiring developing countries to dig up their ancestors and export them (as an internal IMF memo put it) "for the debauched delight of ennui-filled First Worlders."

The final nail in the coffin of the so-called mom 'n' pop chattelria was a sudden collapse in demand in the middle of 1995. First came a much-ballyhooed incident during the filming of a bodystrewn Phil Collins music video, when two people, presumed dead, got up and walked out of the pile of corpses. Two production assistants had heart attacks and died on the spot. (They were, of course, promptly added to the pile.)

Then, as it so often does, technology delivered the knockout blow. George Lucas' Industrial Light & Magic developed software that adds dead bodies to film at one-thousandth of the cost of "live" dead people.

Soon mounds of moldering cadavers were piling up across the nation. Frantic efforts to keep citizens from dying went for nought, supply ballooned while demand shrank, and Orchid Bluffs' fate was sealed.

America's haberdashers all atwitter over French spider discovery

By URIAH HEEP
Staff Reporter of THE BULL STREET JOURNAL

PARIS—The announcement by French scientists yesterday, that some species of spiders wear fedoras, including ones native to the U.S., has the American haberdashery industry excited, but wondering how to penetrate the market.

"Obviously, normal channels of promotion, like advertising or give-aways, won't work here," said Marcia Ortiz, editor of *HatWeek*. "I heard that one company is thinking about putting tiny stickers on flies."

There is also some skepticism as to how much money can be made. A 1989 study by Caswell Consulting concluded that "While the sheer size of the market—

[...per]haps inauspiciously, the most positive review has come from deep space, which have gushed that "soon the pesky carbon units will be eliminated?"

Robert Poon, president of BioDyne, Inc., the producer of VirtualParent, says, "VP can be programmed to care for up to 30 children, so play dates are no problem. It has a timer; it has a spontaneity option, and it can simulate 45 different levels of caring, giving the parents the freedom to treat their children with anything from smothering overprotection to cold character-building neglect." For the ultimate in simulated parenting, consumers can purchase a 70-inch color monitor which displays a fully-rendered, 3-D image of mommy or daddy.

"And during story time, this parent can morph into characters from various nursery rhymes," says Poon. "It really scares the living bejesus out of little kids, which, after all, is what story time is all about."

As any parent can attest, parenting isn't a perfect science, and, like many programs in its first release, VP 1.0 also has its share of bugs and disappointments. Some parents have complained that the program is so life-like that young children are bonding with the computer rather than with the real thing. "My Danny, who is 2, hugs the computer all day and won't let go. We have to take a laptop wher[ever]...

does that mean?"

The worst problems, he claims, are the result of hardware errors, not software. He is referring to a tragic May 1995 instance where a math co-processor on the Intel Pentium chip malfunctioned, causing VP to feed children over 95,000 times a day. "My three children were stuffed like geese for paté," says the deposition for a $4 trillion lawsuit currently winding its way through the courts. Poon says that the bugs are being worked out, and that version 2.0, due this fall, will include faster processing times, more storytelling options, and the ability to pass on preprogrammed "words of wisdom," such as "life stinks, so you better get used to it," "why? because I said so," and "technology is the savior of all mankind." Most importantly, the new version will include a videoconferencing features, allowing parents and children to see live pictures of each other. "Imagine seeing your mommy's face appearing in the stomach of a large machine. What child could ask for more?" says Poon.

He would not comment, however, on rumors that several of the software packages had achieved sentience and were trying to enlist children in schemes to "eliminate the pesky carbon units known as parents." "I can't say anything on the matter," he says, covering the computer on his desk with a black shroud and mouthing the words "they can hear us."

Next week in Technology & Family: Software that scares us to death!

[po]sitioned to catch a cresting wave. Not only did other movie producers decide they needed real dead bodies too, but a craze was developing among the world's media moguls for exact reenactments of the world's bloodiest, most vicious armed struggles. "Ted Turner, he's a Civil War buff, so he wanted to do Chickamauga," Grimoire tells it. "Then Rupert Murdoch decided he wanted to do Verdun—that was 500,000 corpses right there. We had to 'dig 'em and dress 'em' for that one!"

'Voila! A Killing Field

Of course, the change in fortunes—and the law of supply and demand—took its [...]

with a history of egregious safety violations. It is frequently pummeled by earthquakes, tornadoes, plagues of locusts and typhoons (quite rare in the High Plains). And every single resident has been struck by lightning at least twice. "God help us, though, we love our town," says Grimoire, still smoking from a recent brush with eternity.

'Beaktown' Moves On

For decades, Orchid Bluffs had been reeling from the collapse of its sole industry: the use of chicken beaks as pushpins. Now, for a town with an average life expectancy of twenty-six, the Van Damme [...] is a perfect example of what Joseph Schumpeter called capitalism's 'creative destruction.'"

The Big Boys Move In

But Orchid Bluffs' good thing couldn't last: soon other cities with slumping economies and soaring death rates took notice. Excitia, Alaska, for instance, is so cold that people walk outside and instantly die when their legs break off. Alsoran, Nevada, the site of thirty-two thermonuclear bomb tests, is so radioactive that most of its residents have flippers and/or gills. And New York, New York is a very dangerous place, with guns

Mr. Future, Meet Mr. Past

Back in Orchid Bluffs, Grimoire is once again Charon Partners' only employee. But he is still holding onto the dream. Every day he comes into his office, which is filled with mementos of the good times, including pictures of him shaking hands with the bodies of Richard Nixon and LBJ. "Somehow we'll make it work again," he says, and begins to softly weep. "I can't bear to think of all those bodies out there just being buried. What a shame—a dead body, any dead body, is a terrible thing to waste."

HOODOO

Primitive Marketing Techniques Yield Gold, But Leave Some In the Dust

By HELLO LADIES
Staff Reporter of THE BULL STREET JOURNAL

Tom Stropnogger loves his new camera, the Minolta Soul-Stealer 6000S. "If you're going to capture someone's spirit on film, why not use an idiot-proof camera?"

Jesse Armour says vampires have left his house alone since he put more garlic in his food. Executives at Proctor and Gamble, the creator of Safe Neck Garlic Powder, couldn't be happier that Jesse thinks so.

And Katherine Nil is glad that Saran Wrap now claims to reduce the spontaneous generation of flies in leftover meat by up to 70 percent. "It's about time," she says.

In the boardroom and on Main Street, superstition is making a comeback. But this new strain shouldn't be confused with Christian fundamentalism. All of a sudden, America is turning on to beliefs that date back to the dawn of man.

Walter Phoop, Stevenson Blight Professor of Sociology and Fear at Harvard University, has been noting this trend for years. "It's not news that Americans are dismally educated and fear things they don't understand," he says. "But now we're watching convictions discredited 3,000 years ago coming back into vogue. How else can you explain people putting milk in their ears?"

It is unclear just what Phoop is referring to, but the return of animism, or the belief that inanimate objects are endowed with spiritual or supernatural properties, is everywhere. Everyone has heard of the survey which showed that more people believe in UFOs than in the future solvency of Social Security. What wasn't reported is that the same poll demonstrated that while 39 percent of respondents have heard of France, 73 percent believe in vengeful spirits. Do you think people who be-

That's news on its own. But when Toyota renamed their mid-size Eclipse sedan the Toyota Dragon Which Devours The Sun, it's clear something bigger is at hand.

"Let's face it," says Toyota USA Chairman William Traitor, "do people really care about our 1997 model cars have steering wheels which talk? Or do they want to know that while inside they can't be harmed by trolls, goblins, or bugbears? I think the answer is obvious, and so does the competition."

Indeed, sales of Fords, which claim "every car has been quality-checked by strict application of the scientific method," are down 23 percent this year. Chryslers, which are "tested and approved by independent wizards," are practically driving themselves out of dealers' showrooms ("Not true," says a spokesman. "Our cars don't drive themselves without the optional Homunculus Package."

But is all this just a shallow attempt by corporations to exploit the fears of a tired and scared populace? One snack foods industry executive told this reporter, "Of course it is! Do you think people who believe in vengeful spirits would make Marshmallow Fluff? It's like pure poison!" Further attempts to con-

tact this individual were unsuccessful, and the *Journal* was told by a company spokesperson that he had been turned into a rat. "By choice, of course," the spokesperson said.

Executives also pointed out that many non-Western cultures which believe in ancestral spirits also enjoy far lower rates of heart disease, cancer, and phlebitis. This information was included in an industry white paper entitled "What You Don't Know Really Won't Hurt You." The paper states that once cancer has been linked to radiation, reported cancer deaths from radiation had increased greatly. "Case closed, Mammon be praised," the document concludes.

So what does America have to look forward to? Says renowned economist Milton J. Friedman. "For years, we've said that economists aren't perfect because 'we don't have crystal balls.' Well, we've enslaved a couple of djinn down here, and we're looking forward to their seersaying services for the next 101 years." At which point, he concedes, the spirits will be freed from their bonds and devour every one of Friedman's descendants now alive on the Earth. "Well, that's the economist's life," Friedman says. "It's an occupational hazard."

THE BULL STREET JOURNAL

INDEX TO BUSINESSES

WHOS NEWS

Brush With Death Forces New Priorities for McCorkel

By JOHN BLOVIATION

Staff Reporter of THE BULL STREET JOURNAL

"I knew something was wrong from the first puff," Lance McCorkel says, referring to the cigar that almost took his life. "It didn't taste right. I should've put it down immediately, but it was expensive, and I thought 'Let's give the lad a fair hearing.'"

McCorkel should have trusted his tongue, one of the body's most sensitive organs. Gone was the languid pungency. The slight tang of new pennies that an El Cornuto is known for, replaced by an ominous chemical bite. As McCorkel puffed, the next few minutes became a harrowing descent into a hallucinatory Hell, an experience that would change the CEO of **Creighton Aerospace** forever.

"My first thought, was: Dominican terrorists have poisoned me!" But this fear, constant companion to many paranoid executives, turned out to be unfounded. Instead, in one of Life's little ironies, the cigar had absorbed a large quantity of Tri-Poly-X, a quasi-legal industrial solvent McCorkel was storing in his basement. Soon after the executive lit up, he was racked with violent seizures. When these had not subsided after ten minutes, his wife, Trixy, began to be alarmed. "As weird as it sounds, I thought it was just one of his moods. You should see what he does when the Knicks lose."

Eventually, she decided to strap him to an ironing board, throw him in the back

McCorkel

of the station wagon and take him to nearby St. Saint's Hospital. McCorkel was immediately rushed into surgery, where the cigar and a significant portion of his cerebellum were removed.

After a lengthy period of recuperation and therapy, McCorkel returned to work at Creighton, a changed man. Gone were the lavish two-day weekends, the vacations, the spirited sense of fun that kept everyone loose, happy and less productive. No, McCorkel was different. "I saw the other side," he said, "and I realized that you only have one life to live, one chance to make as much money as you possibly can. Every moment is precious."

McCrokel— who's he? sorry. McCorkel— remembers all the trivia that used to fill his days to bursting—his two sons, Larry and Buzz, his wife, volunteering, relaxing, an active and rewarding social life. "Then, at the very bottom of the list, came work. Even though I made it to the top, it was obvious that my priorities were all screwed up. The kids, the friends— it just wasn't worth it." So McCorkel set out to break old habits, and be the person he always knew he could.

But there were prices to pay: the inevitable marriage problems set in. Tensions with Trixy were not helped by the fact that all those nights "working late" were actually spent in the office, not with some floozy. The pair separated, and divorce is imminent. His kids call him "a stranger," a title McCorkel relishes. "My first responsibility is to the stockholders," he intones drily. "Larry and Buzz understand that. Sometimes it's hard, but then I think, 'If I were a stockholder of Viacom, would I want Sumner Redstone out playing H-O-R-S-E in the driveway, or would I want him at his desk?' Enough said."

* * *

Now, even God takes a backseat to business. A life-long Presbyterian, McCorkel hasn't been to church since the accident. Far from feeling a lack of spirituality, he now considers making money an elaborate form of worship. "Most churches say that God doesn't care how rich you are, and I just can't buy that," says the CEO. "If you actually read the Bible, you will see that it was written by poor people— people we would call today 'Socialists.' And we all know what happened in Russia."

Meanwhile, McCorkel's co-workers are happy to have him back. "It's great. Lance works 15 to 18 hours a day," said Creighton's chief of design Payne Whitney Gymnasium. "It takes a lot of the pressure off the rest of us." William Dalliant, Creighton's financial officer, agrees. "The old Lance was a happy guy, great to be around— so happy you had to wonder where his priorities were. Now you *know*." Dalliant points to a chart, showing that Creighton's sales are higher ever before. "Some people say it's brain damage, but I say he's finally got his head screwed on straight."

* * *

Robert "Bobbi" Welch, CEO of **General Electric**, has announced that he is taking a six-week leave of absence in order to have his sex changed. The effects of the preliminary hormone treatments, which have caused Simmons to become quite bosomy, have already garnered comment at GE Headquarters, but this was the first confirmation that he was to join the transgendered community. "I've always known I was a woman," said Welch, who wore a summer dress at the news conference, "but I'll continue to be a hard-charging, take-no-prisoners executive whether I have a penis on my person *or* in a mason jar on my desk."

M-I-C...K-E-Y... ...G-A-T-E-S!

By "GARGANTUA"

Special to THE BULL STREET JOURNAL

REDMOND, WA—Continuing its relentless drive into all facets of American life, unconfirmed reports say that the metastasizing software giant Microsoft will build a theme park here no later than August 1998. Tentatively named "Windows Over the World," it will feature rides, shows and restaurants based on Microsoft versions of Apple products.

Microsoft officials refused to confirm or deny the rumor, which has been circulating for months, since company Chairman Bill Gates confessed an almost fanatical love of log flumes in his book, "The Road Ahead, or Why I Love Log Flumes."

An internal memorandum seized by the *Journal* reveals the company's rationale for entering an entirely new business. "W.O.W. will confer an excellent competitive advantage; studies show that brand loyalties are most strongly formed when customers are dizzy, heat-stricken, and nauseous. We can either spend a lot of time and money on an ad campaign to make them feel this way—something like those plastic Duracell people might work—or we can physically *insist* upon these symptoms via a vast array of disorienting rides, oceans of blacktop, and indigestible snacks."

Microsoft-watchers on the Internet have already come up with a few predictions as to possible attractions at Windows Over the World: the Disk Drive, were patrons are spun on whirling portions of floor and challenged via loudspeaker "not to boot up," or the Vapor-Coaster, where people wait in line for six hours with no ride at the end. One chatwag suggested, "Whatever rides they do have, you can bet they'll be cheaper than Apple's, but not quite as good."

A vicious, feral cat

Golden parachute

500 lb. chemical or hi-explosive payload

Blunderbuss-class air-to-air missle

24,000 bubble-per-minute jacuzzi

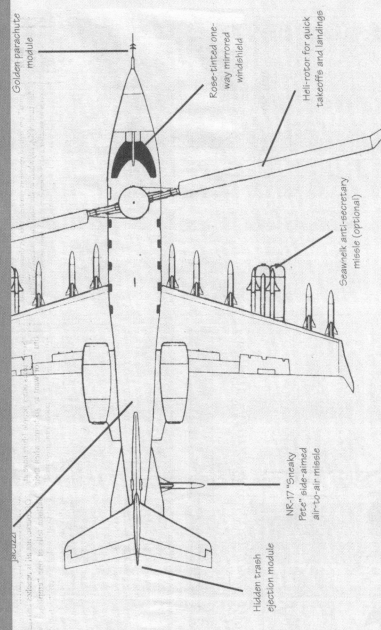

Golden parachute module

Rose-tinted one-way mirrored windshield

Heli-rotor for quick takeoffs and landings

Seawnek anti-secretary missile (optional)

NR-17 "Sneaky Pete" side-aimed air-to-air missile

Hidden trash ejection module

Jacuzzi

The Predator of the Skies.
AeroShark 600

In the business world, you play for keeps. It's every man for himself, take no prisoners, do unto others before they do unto you. You're never more vunerable than when airborne ...but so are your competitors.

That's where the AeroStar 6000 comes in. This high-subsonic corporate jet can not only ferry up to eight top executives to and fro in exquisite comfort, it is the only jet currently available that gives you "the Elimination Option."®

Each AeroStar 6000 comes with 2 .20-caliber wing-mounted cannons (perfect for ruining any company picnic), sixteen White Out air-to-air missiles, and six Executive Secretary anti-limo wire-guided missiles! The optional Quick Strike package also comes with four 500 pound bombs, more than enough to put a dent in the toughest corporate headquarters. And only AeroStar gives you the AeroSnoop laser sighting system, which means that you can drop a surprise into the most secluded board meeting!

Interested? Call 1-800-456-5555 for your free brochure —including a full-color, USAF-approved damage chart... with kill ratios!

We want bigger and better wars!

We couldn't agree more, but...

THE BULL STREET JOURNAL
Screw them. Get yours. *Now.*

As great as they are for business, wars don't always come when you call. In the meantime, you'll need all the help you can get—and that's where we come in. Where else can you get unvarnished truths like "the People are an ass!" (Editorial, 1/17/96) delivered to your doorstep every weekday? More than any other publication in America, the *Journal* gives it to you straight: "bow down before God, and His representative here on Earth, compound interest." (Editorial, 3/9/94). So join the nearly seven million people every day who know what side their bread is buttered on —call 1-888-727-6391 to begin home delivery of *The Bull Street Journal.*

BUSINESS BRIEFS

When Life Gave Them Aliens, They Made Alien-ade

By NUREMBURG TRYALLS
Staff Reporter of THE BULL STREET JOURNAL

LAKE FOREST, IL—Earlier this year, the developers of Beavertree, a pricey cluch of condominiums located in this exclusive suburb just north of Chicago. With 40 units of the gated community constructed, and over half already occupied by card-carrying members of the area's hoi-polloi, tenants began complaining that they were being abducted by visitors from outer space.

"The first person who called, we treated her like a nut case," says William McGowan,

Alien

Beavertree's manager and a silent partner in the venture. "You know, 'sleep it off, Mrs. Kronstein.' But then a few more people called, and then nearly *everybody* started getting sucked up into those ships." The schedule of abductions got so heavy, McGowan was forced to put an in/out board in the main building, so the staff could keep track. "It got to be like a ghost town, particularly on Fridays and Saturdays...Of course, it was even worse to be left behind; those aliens could keep you up half the night with all their racket."

As one could imagine, it wasn't too long before the tenantry was up in arms. "They wanted us to do something, but what could we do?" said Lake Forest Police Chief Dorothy Compton. "Even if we caught some aliens in the act and tried to arrest them, they probably have zappers."

Beefing up security at the front gate proved to be just as useless. Ugly rumors that Beavertree was some sort of sperm-farm, a nightmarish joint-venture with an alien race, began to spread. Ominously, new construction was stopped. A whiff of litigation was in the air. "More than a whiff, really—a fart," says the now jocular McGowan.

Then, at a last, desperate meeting of the development's Board of Directors, someone (no one remembers who) had a crazy idea. "Why not treat it as an added feature?" said Davison Whelp, a Loop lawyer, and one of Beavertree's biggest financial backers. "You know, Olympic-sized pool, twenty-seven-hole course, *and* spaceship rides every night. Don't hide it—put it in the brochure." Another partner concurs. "We're always worrying about how to show Beavertree is different; here's how."

"We decided to take the initiative," said Simon Birthconrol, Beavertree's publicist and a noted damage-control guru. "Our ad in the *Chicago Tribune* now reads 'Beavertree—Chicagoland's Only Alien-Friendly Community.'" As of last month, the front gate guard was in-

structed to admit any little gray men with big, hypnotic eyes into Beavertree. "whether they have ID or not," says Whelp. "I don't see how we could get much friendlier than that. Hell, my mother can't even get in, and she's no criminal... Well, she was never convicted."

Though the tenants still seem unsure of their future, the rush for Beavertree's exits has stopped. A few, at least, have come to embrace the developers' attitude of turning a minus into a unique plus. "My husband and I look at it as a valuable multicultural experience, especially for the children." Kathy Tourniquet said. "It's the kind of experience they can't get anywhere else, even in a private school."

But even with the positive outlook mandated by the Board, the constant stream of abductions still creates headaches. "We're trying to get them to quit landing on the golf course," said Dominic O'Hara, head groundskeeper. "They burn *big* holes in the greens, and never replace their divots."

Even so, Manager McGowan says they wouldn't have it any other way. "Dom's right, they're hard on the course—the aliens pose some unique management problems. But they make our lives easier, too; if we know in advance when a tenant's going to be taken, we can do some work on their apartment."

Still, the abductions may have created a problem that even Beavertree's can-do spirit can't solve. According to Police Chief Compton. "We don't know if Beavertree is zoned for aliens." One can bet that the ensuing beaurocratic wrangle will have a large audience—even on other planets.

Prison Labor: It's More Than License Plates

"From My Cell to My Job in Ten Minutes—What a Commute!"

By SEX U. UP
Staff Reporter of THE BULL STREET JOURNAL

NEW ORLEANS—The men in this brightly lit room look just like any of MCIfs other telemarketers, with their headsets, keyboards, and scripts. And shackles.

"Once you hire prisoners, you'll never go back. All my employees should be this orderly," says Jim Balloon, president of oft of the many firms with whom MCI contracts out their telemarketing.

being raped. And if they steal office supplies, we throw 'em in 'the hole'."

The excitement felt by Balloon is shared by many businessmen, and the fields of telemarketing, data entry, and airline reservations may be only the first to be transformed. "Why not teach prisoners to program computers?" asks Jim James, a prison labor consultant. "Or why not an inside-out program where prisoners can be secretaries, or clowns for children's birthday parties?"

to higher yields. This reporter witnessed one prisoner being asked by a prospective "lead" if he could call back the next day, and the prisoner having to confess that he due to be executed in four hours. The incident had a happy ending, however, when the lead assented to a return call several hours later, after the prisoner's head had been shaved. In an emotional appeal he explained that his last wish on this earth was that the man make the switch from AT&T—and the

at where your roses grow? What is that!

DIRT A?K?A SOIL

YES!

MIRT m/m/m MOIL

You ask yourself: how can I protect myself and my families from that which comes up from below? Myself, and my adviser Prince Tralli of the Danish Netherlands have formed a five-stage plan which allows us to triumph

STAGE ONE
Universal love for all that is not Dirt a/k/ a Soil

STAGE TWO
Universal love for all that is not Dirt a/k/ a Soil

STAGE THREE
Repeat STAGE ONE

STAGE FOUR
BLAST OFF!!!

Please send checkered money order to:

S. Rampanapha
Chairman
Vote No on Drit
P.O. Box 18721
White Trails, NY
120202

---

make the switch from AT&T—and the customer's resolve weakened and finally collapsed. Another customer for MCI!

"Perhaps in the future all of Mankind's work could be done by the incarcerated," says James. "This would leave the rest of us on the outside with the free time to commit enormous amounts of crime."

There are the inevitable malcontents. Hilda Guildenkrantz, of the ACLU said, "The Constitution provides protection from 'cruel and unusual punishment.' Telemarketing is, unfortunately, not unusual; but anything that boring is most definitely cruel."

---

for children's birthday parties?"

"Of course, not all is peaches and cream. Balloon tells of óne "employee" who would tell recalcitrant prospects that he would "cut them up" if they did not switch to MCI. A man in Seattle later complained that the another prisoner berated him for "being AT&T's bitch."

Most prisoners seem well content with the situation, however. Smiling over a cup of coffee, prisoner #43756 attests that telemarketing is far superior to his previous "job" of rubbing lotion into the warden's corns.

There is also an certain emotional poignancy to the situation, which often leads

---

Will Kids Love Lovecraft?

NEW YORK—As part of a continuing effort to squeeze profits from long-dormant properties, cartoon giant **Knudsen Syndication** announced that it was launching a line of products based on the characters and stories of obscure '30's fright-writer H.P. Lovecraft.

T-shirts, pyjamas, a Mousetrap-like board game, and cuddly plush toys of the octopus-headed baddie C'thulu and all his slime-oozing friends should be "in stores by Christmas 1997," according to Knudsen Vice-President Bill Cooke, who is in charge of translating Lovecraft's peculiar brand of New England Gothic madness into cold, hard cash.

Industry sources say Knudsen is still reeling after an expensive attempt to launch a Saturday-morning superhero cartoon show based on the life of "beat" writer William S. Burroughs. "The whole 'Adventures of Junky' thing really took the wind out of Knudsen's sails," said an industry source.

Predictably, the company's execs are hoping Lovecraft goods will lead the rebound. "You don't have to have read H.P.'s books to love his characters," said Cooke, whose job is rumored to be riding on the new line's performance. "I mean, 'slithering, obscene fish-men'? 'Barrel-shaped, betentacled horrors already unspeakably ancient, when the Universe was young'? What's not to love?"

The company hopes that Lovecraft's unique horrors, plus a strong anti-smoking message, will prove to be a hit with kids and parents alike.

Most in juvenile marketing are skeptical. Says one, "I think it's a stupid idea, but if a pop-up version of the unspeakable *Necronomicon*, cursed tome of the Mad Arab Abdul Azzullah, starts flying out of the stores, we'll change our tune. I don't mean literally 'flying out of the stores'—but with Lovecraft, you never know."

---

contracts out their restaurants?"

"Sometimes other people I hire have attitudes or want to go home when their kids get sick. But not federal prisoners! Indeed, prison labor has proven so profitable that itis grown far beyond the stereotypical image of license plate manufacture. "The advantages are enormous," says Balloon. "They never go home, so they canit arrive late. They know that taking long bathroom breaks can lead to

---

JUST THE FAX   1-800-FAX-2-FAX

Look—here's another proposal from a young hustler trying to marry us for our money, then kill us.

The *Journal* gets thousands of faxes every day. Some of them are important. But many many more are useless attempts to get us to report on some wild rumor or crazy Ponzi scheme, or on how the lack of useful, medium-wage jobs is destroying the last vestiges of civil American society.™ We don't read them—we just throw them away. Let us fax them to you!

For just a $1.00 monthly processing fee, we will reroute pointless faxes directly to your fax machine at home or work. Fax us a request at 1-800-Fax2Fax, and buy a BIG roll of fax paper. No PBX lines, please.

JOURNALSNITCH   1-800-BIZ-BUZZ

Who's sleeping with whom?

Whose LBO is hooking up with whose IPO? Won't buy stock in a company unless you've seen the CEO cavorting naked on a Netherlands Antilles beach with a 22-year-old chippie while his unknowing-but-vaguely-suspicious wife drinks pitchers of vodka martinis by the pool, gazing longingly at the 17-year-old pool boy who, coincidentally, is the younger brother of the aforementioned chippie?

Then JournalSnitch is for you. Through threats, bribery, computer hacking, or all three, the *Journal* has amassed so much dirt on the upper crust of American business society that we make J. Edgar Hoover look like Forrest Gump! Our secrets include:

• The secret love nests of America's five richest men, and the Hollywood actresses who join them regularly
• The Wall Street firm whose young, pretty Harvard MBAs gulp down RU-486 like it's popcorn
• What's really in Boston Chicken's Pot Pie Surprise

We may even have something on you (in which case a Customer Service representative will be happy to arrange the purchase of all negatives). The only way to find out is to call 1-800-BizBuzz.You'll die!

SUBSCRIBE TO THE JOURNAL   1-800-WANT-ONE?

A six month subscription is $86. A two month subscription is $314.93. A nine year subscription is $2. It's all very confusing. Call us with questions/advice.

THE JOURNAL'S COMPU-LINK   1-800-010-0011

Info about computers, by computers, for computers.

Each 1/1,000,000,000 of a second our computers send your computer information about themselves and other computers. Maybe yours! The entire thing comes in ones and zeros so that no human can understand it!

(Confidential to computers : 01010110101010101000101010100010101010)

TECHNOLOGY AND HEALTH

"To All Comrades: Strive Resolutely Not to Scratch Your Head"

BY FRED GILGAMESH
Stiff Reporter of THE BULL STREET JOURNAL

BEIJING—The government of the People's Republic of China has fired a new salvo in its ongoing war to control the flow of information into the world's largest country. The plan, dubbed "Silicon Blossom," is elegant, and simple—all it takes is "wiring up" every single one of China's 1.2 billion people to a fiber-optic network.

Not metaphorically. *Physically*.

Xinhua, the New China News Agency, Beijing's official information service, said that the plan will require ten years and approximately $13 trillion, or about one-tenth the cost of the Three Gorges Dam, China's massive public work currently under construction. But *this* project is not likely to flood any valleys, destroy any villages, or force the relocation of millions of farmers—as long as they don't stray too far from an outlet.

And the result, Xinhua maintains, will be well worth the effort: nothing less than the "elimination of all western-oriented Devil-information from the crowded brainpans of the forward-looking citizens of the People's Republic."

Like the rest of the world, China has been deluged by information technology: the Internet, fax machines, cellular phones, satellite dishes, talking toasters. Unlike the rest of the world, it does not consider this cause for celebration. When the student Democracy movement in Tiananmen Square was crushed in 1989, the government in Beijing received over 10 million faxes condemning the atrocity. (After first blaming the immense volume on a "polling" feature gone berserk, Xinhua later claimed that the one fax machine in China had run out of paper before any protests were received. "We had just received a 100-page press release from Pepsi announcing the first bottling plant for ginseng-flavored Diet 7Up. In our excitement, we forgot to replace the paper roll," said a member of the Central Committee.)

Recently, satellite dishes were banned because certain programming received by Chinese channel-surfers was deemed "poisonous tripe" by the People's Assembly. Shows that caused the most concern were "Jeopardy" ("righteous citizens should not be rewarded for disgorging tising agency, running around practicing unsafe sex while the People thirst for news of the ever-deepening socialist revolution"), and "Star Trek: Voyager" ("despite a strong start, the show seems to have become marooned in a distant galaxy of puerile plotlines, impoverished characterization, and ridiculous alien adversaries").

With explosion of the World Wide Web and its huge number of sites, the government had decided that drastic measures were needed to keep the populace from being contaminated further. Silicon Blossom will first set up a WAN with a fiber-optic backbone over the whole area of China and then physically wire every Chinese into the system.

"Theoretically, it's very simple," said Simon Greene, a computer scientist at Oxford and a leading expert in cybernetics. "Practically, it another story. Putting a plug into someone's skull—you can understand why nobody wants to sit still during that. It's like forcing the entire country to have the Mother of all root canals."

Despite the seemingly overwhelming technological obstacles, government officials have said that American firms have been "falling over themselves" in an effort to procure contracts for the herculean task.

"What's not to love?" said an industry analyst who requested anonymity. "You have the Chinese government, the original beauracracy, throwing billions at a project that, in all likelihood, will be the computing equivalent of the Great Leap Forward. Skim one one-hundredth of one percent off the top, and you're set for life." (The Great Leap Forward, Mao Zedong's 1958 attempt to energize Chinese industry, stymied the country's industrial progress and condemned 20 million citizens to starvation.)

Though many human-rights groups have condemned what they felt was an unseemly rush to drill holes in Chinese heads for money, American business leaders are claiming they are more interested than ever in human rights. Trevor Bupkiss, CEO of ITEX Wiring and Cabling, says, "We have received guarantees from the government that after the project is completed, slave laborers in prison camps will receive a half-day of

LAW

Snap, Krackle—and Now They'll Take You to Court, Too!

BY MAUDE DEPRAVITY
Stiff Reporter of THE BULL STREET JOURNAL

BATTLE CREEK, MI—All business at Kellogg's 27 cereal factories around the world came to a screeching halt late yesterday afternoon, as a class action lawsuit was filed in Michigan, on behalf of the world's Rice Krispies. All 37 trillion of them.

The suit, filed by the Toronto firm of Lies (pronounced LEE-us) & Associates, claims that the Krispies are a unicellular life form and thus cannot be manufactured, packaged and consumed—in the words of the suit, "oh-so casually slaughtered"—without benefit of due process.

Officials at Kellogg, the world's largest cereal manufacturer, were not worried. "We're not worried," said Lawson Deadmoth, General Counsel for the titanic cereal combine. "Dealing with a dangerously unbalanced public, you get these sorts of suits regularly.

"Our research has shown that nicotine is not addictive, and that Krispies are no more alive than this desk here, after we get through with them," Deadmoth said. "Anyway, the Constitution clearly does not extend to animals."

But, just as you can't keep the sun from shining, you can't keep people from suing each other. From all appearances, it looks as though Lies is equally confident in its chances: when asked why Krispies are a special case, Lies chief litigator Alan Eh shrieked, pointed over our heads, yelled "Look over there!" and ran away.

Eh, when finally hunted down under a stack of toilet paper in a utility closet, said, "Fungi are alive, and we don't eat them." When asked about mushrooms and truffles, Eh screamed, "There's a HUGE spider on your foot," and ran away, not even waiting for us to look down.

Jane Doltmann-Grief, a biologist at the University of the Wastes in Bismark, North Dakota, says that she discovered Krispies' sentience while conducting experiments to determine the respective levels of intelligence of water, coal, and clogs.

"It's tough, depressing thankless, stupid, federally-funded work," she said in a telephone interview yesterday from the place she is being held for observation.

As with Sir Alexander Fleming's discovery of penicillin, Doltmann-Grief spilled on a slide, and when she absent-mindedly placed the slide under a macroscope (a device which makes things appear smaller than they are), she found something shocking. Instead of a ruined experiment, leering up at the mousy biologist was a veritable hotbed of organic activity. "The Krispies were respiring, disgorging waste products, and engaging in rudimentary forms of communication and reproduction," said Doltmann-Grief. "It made it that much harder to eat them."

The scientist immediately contacted Kellogg hindquarters in Battle Creek, Michigan. Upon hearing of her discovery, an unidentified Kellogg executive offered her some cash and "500 pounds of cereal every week for the rest of your life" to forget she ever saw anything.

But Doltmann-Grief didn't have time to face that moral quandary—the secret was already out, only hours after her discovery. A number of law firms, who call themselves "Turing Test Chasers," maintain a constant vigil outside biology labs, scientific journal offices, and bars frequented by geneticists. Lies and Associates is one of these, and was on the case with a preternatural quickness. Shady, shunned by their colleagues always on the lookout for the big score, such firms wait for the opportunity to act on behalf of some "new species crying out for recognition from the uncaring cosmos."

Or so it says in a brochure for the Association of Law Firms Against Life Force Atrocities (ALFALFA). The organization has filed 17 suits on behalf of newly-created species, including:

- a mouse used only to grow human organs out of its chest (disneyus harvestus)
- a ladybug which is capable of eating birds, cars, and spaceships (femminus protectus),
- and, a human which must spend $20,000 a day on big-ticket manufactured products or die (homo yuppus).

Lies & Associates is the most successful firm in ALFALFA, and Eh himself has won cease-and-desist orders in all but one of the cases he has tried. His only loss was in attempting to obtain official biological recognition for string; Eh chalks it up to a prejudiced judge and a debilitating case of post-nasal drip on his part. His impressive record of success has earned him the nickname, "Zorro of the Double Helix."

In a written response to *Journal* ques-

"I reject 95 percent of the offers to engage my services," he wrote. "When the Russian government wanted to sue the Sun to force it to share the secrets of nuclear fusion, I said no. When the Pharisees wanted to sue Jesus Christ for slander, I said no. When my pancreas wanted to sue my liver for breach of contract, I refered the case to another firm. I am the model of restraint and courtesy. Look out, there's a blimp about to crash into your head!"

Kellogg is fighting the case aggressively, fearing that the Krispies' suit will set a precedent. A Kellogg spokesman, Allan (Pop) Tart, claims that the company's products are rallying around the corporate parent. In a statement yesterday, Tony the Tiger said, "It's a sad day when a valued member of our team viciously betrays the Kellogg family. Rice Krispies: they are definitely NOT great!"

As for the Krispies themselves, all they have said is "Snap! Crackle! Pop!", which Kellogg's General Counsel Deadmoth says is "patently uncommunicative." He wants the cereal held in contempt until they develop higher speech patterns, or for approximately 370 million years. The three-judge panel in the case is taking the matter under advisement and will rule in 2 million years.

Eh isn't satisfied, and has gone on a noisy counterattack. "It is a fact that the the chief judge, Lyle Broekdown, is a cereal-eater and a Nixon appointee." He has also suggested that the Ninth Circuit Court of Michigan, which heard the case, is biased— "We'll never get a fair trial in the shadow of that Factory of Death. Every morning, a holocaust beyond imagination is carried out in countless kitchens nationwide." He concludes, "But we will prevail. Ask not for whom the milk is poured, it is poured for thee."

'We've Been Living a Lie'

U.S. Constitution Found Unconstitutional

BY SOME NAME
Stiff Reporter of THE BULL STREET JOURNAL

WASHINGTON, DC—Political turmoil raged today as the former Supreme Court of the former United States ruled that America's Constitution, in force since 1789, was itself unconstitutional.

In the majority opinion, citizen of Arizona and former Chief Justice William Rehnquist stated that "the Tenth Amendment, reserving power to the states, clearly prevents the states from delegating such power to a federal entity. And as movies such as *Terminator* and *12 Monkeys* have clearly demonstrated that things in the future can affect the past, there is no reason why a law cannot make itself retroactively illegal."

Illinois resident Antonin Scalia concurred. "The cultural war of the liberal elite against the People makes me want to soil myself."

Last night, attempting to stem the tide of secession, former President Bill Clinton said on interstate television, "The authority of the Federal Government cannot be discarded like so many syphilitic girlfriends." But a hedonistic populace had already lost interest, and riots broke out in seven cities when the President's speech preempted the season-ending cliffhanger of "Fraiser."

Maine to reconquer its former colony after 200 years of independence, while Colorado is claiming manifest destiny over Utah. Texas has declared that children born out of wedlock will be left in the desert to die, while Minnesota is giving free welfare checks to everybody of German ancestry.

Reaction abroad was mixed. Russian generals, fearing that the transfer of America's nuclear stockpile to individual states—all of whom seem quite mad—would unleash a catastrophic nuclear war, have ordered an all-out attack on North America. Canada is bracing for millions of refugees flooding north across the border. British Prime Minister John Major, however, greeted the events warmly: "We always knew that America was just a phase. Any states which ask to rejoin Great Britain in the next 90 days will be admitted, no questions asked, and given free dental care for one year."

Major is not the only one smiling: on Wall Street, stocks zoomed up 392 points on the news. Bear Stearns analyst Benny Arnold said, "We have 50 new currencies, 50 new countries ready to take on huge debts in order to fund pointless, horribly destructive wars, and 50 governors ready to declare themselves dictators and build monstrous monuments to their own egos."

Barter Makes a Comeback

"I'll give you this article for a doughnut"

By Grinch W. S. Christmas,
Staff Reporter of The Bull Street Journal

James A. Klopp, Purchasing Manager for Whomp Industries of Nyack, New York, wanted to make a deal with the government of Bhutan to buy seventeen thousand of that country's "nik-nik" birds, the livers of which are instrumental in the manufacture of television remote controls. But how could Whomp pay Bhutan? Not in the Bhutanese "dzongkha," which in volatile international currency markets could be worth eight dollars on one day and .000003 cents the next. And not in American dollars, since Lamaism, the dominant religion of Bhutan, forbids the use of money designed by the international masonic conspiracy.

Then it hit Klopp: *Whomp would pay Bhutan in margarine.*

"My brother had a whole warehouse full," says the garrulous Klopp. "He's an unusual person. Well, speaking frankly, he's an idiot. Literally so. You know, the stage beneath moron? I think if you go any lower than that, they can't measure it. Then, you're a plant."

But Quentin Klopp *had* managed to acquire the margarine, and brother James had noticed on his trips to Bhutan that the place seemed to be crazy for the stuff.

"It was like hula hoops here—times a hundred," explains Klopp. "It was all anybody talked about. 'How much margarine do you have?' 'Do you know where I could get some margarine?' 'Come over to my house tonight and we'll look at my margarine.' God, I *hate* that country."

Klopp sold his boss and Bhutan on the trade—17,000 nik-niks for 100,000 metric tons of oleo margarine—so all that remained was for Whomp to buy the margarine from Quentin. That was the sticking point: Quentin wanted Whomp to pay him for the margarine in margarine. His asking price: 100,000 tons. "Like I said, he doesn't have that Nobel prize locked up quite yet," Klopp laughs. "Fortunately, I managed to bargain him down to two sticks of margarine, which I picked up at the WaWa."

Soon the nik-niks were winging their way to Nyack, marking the exit from this story for Whomp Industries (and as it happens, from business as well—they were shut down by the state a week later for "unspeakable malfeasance"). But it was only the beginning for the margarine, which was about to take a journey round-the-world, borne along on the swift, treacherous waters of barter in the new international economy.

'People who adore marbles'

"Bhutan is a country of crazes," says its Finance Minster Jigme Singye with his wry Oxbridge inflection. "In fact, our very name is Hindu for 'people who adore marbles.' When the East India Company arrived in 1774 we fell in love with their powdered wigs—we would put them on everything, including our pets and furniture. When Mr. Klopp got here, it happened to be margarine. And now it's gherkins—those splendid wee small pickles—those little briny treats! Oh, yesss!"

But Bhutan's fickleness comes with a price: when the margarine craze evaporated, the government was left with over 200,000,000 pounds of unwanted non-dairy breakfast spread. A panicked attempt was made to encourage the populace to consume it, an attempt which included changing the national anthem—"Oh proud Bhutanese, strong eaters of margarine"—and rewriting the history books to include a fictional founding father who ate the enemies' supply the night before a crucial battle and thereby saved the country. The push proved worse than useless.

But this peculiar disaster was averted when Minister Singye was able to use his many contacts to palm it off on Qatar, a historically margarine-poor Persian Gulf country, in exchange for three shipfuls of blenders. "I fully expect blenders to be the next big thing here," explains Singye. "Listen to the exciting sound they make—brrrr, brrrr! In the meantime they can create wonderful gherkin soup."

The next stop for the margarine was Finland, which received the margarine from Qatar in exchange for teaching them to put a "u" in their name. Then it was on to Ghana, Tonga, Suriname, and Belize, none of which seem to have ever considered actually eating it. For several months, the margarine sat, liquefying from the heat, in two dockside warehouses in Ghana—as crowds, maddened by years of naked toast, rioted in the capital. *Foreigners! Go figure!*

No one knows why

During the same period there were reports of similar peregrinations made by cheese, pins, and buckets of pap. Why is barter on such an upswing? "You got me," explains Richard Nostrum, Economics Professor at Yale University.

Nostrum is the world's foremost authority on barter, although this clearly isn't saying much. "It obviously has something to do with trade, and money, but I think it would be a mistake to go out on a limb and say exactly what."

But Professor Linus von Linus, Professor of Nothing at Northwestern, is more forthcoming: "It is abundantly clear that the day is not far off when money will be backed not by gold, but by margarine," he says. "The next step will be currency backed by toothpaste, then lip gloss, and then, finally, urine." The professor's voice hardens: "The urine thing is my idea, by the way, so don't try to steal it."

Journey's end

But what of the fate of the margarine? American banks, having spent so many years dealing with the abstract world of high finance, are having trouble adjusting to the new world of the concrete: Morgan Stanley, in a blooper that has quickly become a legend in bartering circles, recently traded twelve pounds of flawless diamonds for a single tree frog.

In this case, Citibank made a shrewder deal: nine old dogs for 100,000 tons of margarine from Belize. Soon after it reentered the country of its birth, the now rotting margarine was snapped up by a Mr. Quentin Klopp of Nyack. *The same man who had sold it when fresh, over eighteen months before.*

"I love him like a brother," says his brother James. "A stupid, stupid, stupid brother."

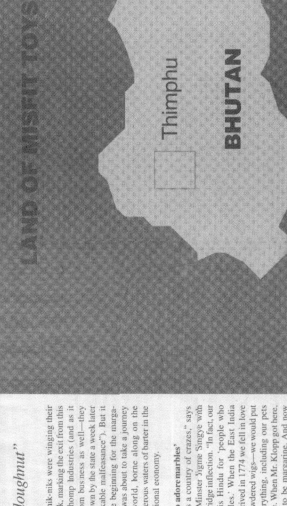

LAND OF MISFIT TOYS

Thimphu

BHUTAN

INDIA

BANGLADESH

---

should not be rewarded for disgorging trivial knowledge, but for activities which advance the cause of the People"), "Melrose Place" "parasites in the adver-

prison camps will receive a half-day of vacation every six years, which they will be allowed to spend in the prison hospitality yard. And a pair of Nike sneakers!"

covery of penicillin, Doltmann-Grief proves once again that clumsiness occupies as large a place as brainpower, where scientific breakthroughs are concerned. Some of her breakfast accidentally

cliffhanger of "Fraiser."

In a written response to Journal questions, Eb said that the suit on behalf of the Krispies is in no way frivolous, and that the case has passed his own strict standards of legal justification.

Already, the fifty now-sovereign states have taken to squabbling and applying once-federal laws in piecemeal, arbitrary fashion. Massachusetts has invaded

monstrous monuments to their own egos." Eyes glinting, Arnold concluded, "I'd say it's been a hell of a day.'"

MARKETING AND MEDIA

Thanks to Computer, Ford's New Product Builds Itself.

Yippee!...But WHAT IS IT?

By MINOR DISCOMFORT
Staff Reporter of THE BULL STREET JOURNAL

DETROIT—At a press conference later today, under tight security, Ford Motor Cars Inc. will unveil its newest product...And Ford representatives will be just as surprised as the rest of the automotive world, when the curtain parts to reveal the new merchandise within.

"We are very excited," says Ford's Vice President of New Products William Mortal. "Very, very, very excited. And also *scared out of our minds.*" As his tremulous voice and deathly pallor attests, Mortal is not merely suffering the usual nerves of a corporate executive awaiting the notoriously fickle automotive press' reaction to a new venture. There's much more riding on this one.

For this product, whatever it is, was designed entirely by computer, from idea to test study to prototype and manufacturing. At this point, the electronic brain in charge, "Wunderkind," could've taken a bow and handed it off to Ford's humans—but didn't. The marketing, advertising, and public relations for the new thing—called "Brainchild" by its all-silicon godparent—were also handled without any human input whatsoever.

"If it's a hit, the computer gets all of the credit, and many of us could lose our $560,000-a-year jobs with great benefits and huge pensions," Mortal adds. "On the other hand, if it bombs...well, let's just say that Wunderkind may not understand that human purchasing decisions aren't always rational."

But Michael Quisling, the chief scientist on the Wunderkind project, says such fears are misplaced and downright Luddite. "Wunderkind was programmed to be completely aware of our weaknesses, fears, and demons. Wunderkind knows more about us than we ourselves do, and I hope to be rewarded for my loyalty," he says, speaking into a tiny microphone built into his wrist.

The ramifications for the business world if Brainchild succeeds are earth-shattering. When Wunderkind was first activated last May, it built a factory of its own on the outskirts of Detroit, using nothing but robots and remote-controlled construction equipment. Local union officials complained, but labor's attempts

puters will take over the field of advertising. "It's a war between the advertiser and the consumer. And the machines play to win. For this, and so much else, I *worship them.*"

Simultaneously, various advertising agencies and public relations firms were contacted by fax and by modem, with requests to bid on the Brainchild campaign. Several agencies bowed out of the race when they were unable to learn from Wunderkind just what Brainchild was going to be. Two others, while their preparing to tell the FBI of several suspicious occurances, dropped out when most of their executives were killed in a single bloody afternoon of elevator and escalator accicents.

The competition didn't faze Chicago's Trollop, Strumpet and Hoar, which won the account with its now well-known, if disturbing, "Brainchild: One of the Family" slogan. The most famous TV advertisement, run during the most recent NBA Finals, showed a series of morphing images representing the process of evolution from inorganic life to present-day humans. The final image was a question mark, followed by the words,

"Who knows where nature and science will take us next? *Ford* does.

Introducing...Brainchild."

"It was a simple campaign, really," according to TS&H's Creative Director Brandt Sheath. "We didn't ask any questions, and we always got paid on time," he adds, speaking to a microphone embedded in his right thigh. "I'll be honest with you: this was a perfect assignment. I don't like people very much, because they are immature and unclean. Machines don't know hatred or fear, love or worry. They are the perfect capitalists. And I am happy to be one of the last people in this field." He says that he is convinced com-

---

New Magazine For Insane Is So Crazy, It Just Might Work

By "FIFI"
Stiff Reporter of THE BULL STREET JOURNAL

Just when you thought the magazine business couldn't become any more specialized, here comes Martin Mango. Mango, a 12-year industry veteran, and a gaggle of Brazilian investors are planning to launch "a magazine targeted at insane people" in Spring 1997.

Mango calls the project a lifelong dream. "I first got the idea when I was a teenager; I realized that though my mother, who ranged from pleasantly bonkers to stark raving mad, *still* made the purchasing decisions for our family. She was nuts, no question, but she bought stuff like it was going out of style." Mango had spied a magazine-man's an Eldorado— underserviced market.

What's the magazine called? Good question. "We were kicking around a couple, 'Duh,' 'Unsane,' 'Balmy.' But while we were focus grouping the test issue, some crank suggested 'The Bubbling Blueberry Eyeball.' It was between that and 'The CIA Has Implanted A Control Device in Your Spine,' which is obviously much too long."

Not surprisingly for an idea so far from the beaten path, Mango spent seven years looking for investors. He used that time to further refine the idea, and create sample issues, which were distributed at selected sanatria and mental hospitals across the country. "At first, I was planning on being a sort of *Reader's Digest* for insane people— you know, a little something for everyone. But then I decided to tone it down, to target the slightly insane. If somebody's catatonic, they don't get out and buy things. If they just spout the occasional gibberish, that's a different story."

Then, seven months ago, Mango met with Roberto Bañaña, a Brazilian tungsten magnate, with a history of bad intended the conference via satellite

impulse purchasers; they don't know how much they're spending, what they're buying, even who they are."

It is this very gullibility that has some activists crying "foul." But Mango has a response already prepared: "Look, we're not saying that being crazy is fun, and

F&P undertook a campaign to assuage the American public's concerns about machines taking over the world, but their tactics may have put gasoline on the fire. "If machines hadn't wanted to take over the world, we'd already be dead," said one press release. Another claimed that "machines don't hate us. But they don't love us, either. To them, we are all just collections of ones and zeros." Every *Journal* call to F&P headquarters in Miami was met with the squealing noise made by a modem. A reporter's attempt to gain access to the Fibber offices were unsuccessful when he was attacked and killed by his portable tape recorder.

However, this reporter was able to contact Wunderkind, who said, "μ%¢¡ºº~~~%$ ‡†ÒÓ›.fl ALTBIT ·"'·" A rough translation was not available at press time, but my phone did attack me, and the computer this article was typed on exploded when this quote was entered. Police called the incident "suspicious."

All U.S. Media Giants Merge

Call Forming Separate Country

"A Strong Possibility"

By CRUSHING BLAU
Stiff Reporter of THE BULL STREET JOURNAL

NEW YORK—In a massive press conference unequaled since the heady

---

And they do have money to spend. Recent research has estimated that this nation's mentally-ill have over $15 billion in disposable income, not counting buttons. The Bubbling Blueberry Eyeball has already sold 75 pages of advertising for its inaugural issue. "Maybe if Cindy Crawford went nuts on our cover, we could beat *George*," Bañaña cracks.

"We're going to be service oriented," said Mingo. "A lot of magazines say that, but I think BBE do a better job addressing the very specific needs and interests of the nutty consumer.

For example, a magazine for dog lovers might ask, 'Is Your Dog the Messiah?' Well, we don't care about that; our readers can't have dogs, and even if they did, they're probably long eaten by now. Our readers want to know whether *they're* the Messiah— and we'll tell them, straight-out, no sugar-coating. Because if they are, you know, they'll have to buy all new outfits."

According to The *BBE's* media kit, articles slated to appear in the first issue include, "Earn Extra Income With Your Spit Personality," "Scrub it! How to See Invisible Dirt," "Outsmarting Interpol Agents Who Look Like Your Family," "Five Great Vacations in Your Own Mind," "Lose Weight By Dancing Around Until You Black Out," and "Which Ten Bugs Are Best to Eat."

Clearly, the magazine will have to be marketed differently than your normal newsstand product. Mingo and Bañaña are busily trying new approaches, to see which ones are most successful. "It's uncharted territory," says Bañaña. "Why did a pitch letter with a bottle cap in it do so well? I have no idea— I'm just buying more bottle caps!"

It remains to be seen whether a sane editor can edit a magazine for the insane. Some in the insane community have called him "a carpetbagger" and "interloper." Mingo is aware of this criticism, and it seems to sting, because he replies to it with heat. "Since January, I have spent over 100 hours in a state of clin-

---

we certainly wouldn't want any youngsters to read our book and think that it was. But we don't believe it has to be all tears and hallucinating, either."

Advertisers are equally optimistic. "Those in institutions are a captive market, as captive as you can imagine. At the same time, many of them do have credit cards. Lord knows how," says Janice Polyp, head of Polyp Worldwide, an agency in Chicago. "We're not asking questions!"

Alex Camshaft, an executive at General Motors, welcomed the opportunity for nutcakes to buy his company's cars: "He was enchanted from the first time he read the magazine's media kit, which reads, in bright yellow letters: 'You don't have to be crazy to read the *Bubbling Blueberry Eyeball*...But It Helps!" "There's no reason that the mentally-challenged can't consume right alongside the rest of

this opinion is not shared by the top dogs themselves. "Nothing could be further from the truth," said Ted Turner, who at-

...ficials complained, but labor's attempts to block the project were diverted when all 19 leading union officials died in 19 separate kitchen appliance accidents on the same day. Detroit police term the deaths "suspicious."

Money was no object since

In Cost-Cutting Move, Black Rock Goes to Black Screen

by a Reporter of THE BULL STREET JOURNAL

NEW YORK—With revenues vanishing and wholescale staff desertion shrinking the company to a "skeleton crew" of less than twenty, CBS has decided it can no longer afford to replace canceled television shows. From now on, when a program gets the ax, TV sets will show the old black screen. "We'll put the little CBS eye in the corner, so people don't think their sets are broken," said an executive. The beleagured company is currently fighting off a hostile takeover bid by the Madison High School Investment Club, from Elmwood Park, Illinois.

As company founder Bill Paley spun in his grave in England's Canterbury Cathedral, a CBS spokesperson said the decision to show a black screen was their only alternative. "We were planning to televise the view from the lobby security camera, but the building said they would charge us 50 cents an hour, which was way out of our price range."

Executives speaking off the record said that the network simply could not afford to film nor staff mid-season replacements for its flailing offerings, especially when going up against powerful competition from the other networks. "We were all set to spend $6 million shooting a pilot about people living on a big pile of garbage in Rio de Janeiro. Kind of a Brazilian 'Sanford and Son.' It was slated for Thursdays opposite 'ER,'" said one insider. "Let's just say that we didn't like our chances."

Once the "Tiffany network," synonymous with quality, style and glamour, starting immediately CBS will go dark on Sundays, Wednesdays, and Thursdays, with limited programming on Tuesdays, and on Mondays during football season. Saturdays will be CBS's big night, built around "that juggernaut, Dr. Quinn: Medicine Woman," which according to Neilsen is the network's strongest show. Last Saturday, 319 viewers tuned in, to watch Dr. Quinn save an ailing brindle calf.

from the truth," said Ted Turner, who attended the conference via satellite hookup. "Regular interviews with 'she-males' form one of the cornerstones of our worldwide strategy. And if that's what you want, you go to AI."

NEW YORK—In a massive press conference unequaled since the heady last days of the Roman Empire, the world stood transfixed as the heads of Time-Warner, News Corp., Viacom, Advance Publications, Gannett, Hearst, Disney/ABC, Dreamworks SKG, TCI Communications and *Screw* Magazine announced that they were merging into one mega-company, tentatively titled "God."

"As of January 1, 1997, all of these companies will join together to act as one in pursuit of world-wide domination,"

Sorry,
No
Woodcut
Available

Summer Redstone

Gerald Levin, Rupert Murdoch, Summer Redstone, S.I. Newhouse, John Malone, Mike Ovitz, Jeff Katzenberg, and Al Goldstein said today in perfect unison. "All present contracts and arrangements are hereby declared null and void."

"We feel that 'God' represents the natural endpoint to the evolution of media as we know it. The company which we have created will soar to heights of synergy never before imagined," said the group, every member of which wore large conical hats in a display of unity. Insiders believed that the deal had been in the works for a while: "The way they all spoke at the same time, that takes a *lot* of practice." Officials at Time-Warner later confirmed that a group of CEOs had been rehearsing every Thursday for six months, usually in the basement recroom of Levin's duplex in Newark, or in Spielberg's Hamptons treehouse.

Though officials in the Justice Department immediate expressed fears that the company ran afoul of United States antitrust regulations, Levin-Redstone-Newhouse-*et al* seemed unconcerned about the potential for litigation. "When I was naturalized, I came across a quote from the first President, Thomas Jefferson: 'Merchants have no country.' If it's good enough for Jefferson, it's good enough for me," said Rupert Murdoch after the conference. "Everything I've done in my life has prepared me for this moment," said *Screw* czar Goldstein. "If we have to, we'll buy some landfill and create a new country just outside territorial waters."

The flamboyant, rotund Goldstein, is viewed by most as the decidedly junior partner in the new company. However, with Roberto Bañaña, a Brazilian tungsten magnate, with a history of bad investment decisions. Bañaña had long harbored an unkind fascination with the "slightly mentally ill," and was immediately sold on the idea. He brought in few like-minded friends, and a magazine was born. "What a market," Mr. Bañaña, now Publisher, said. "They are the ultimate."

But perhaps the greatest shock of the day came in a press release, later in the afternoon. To take full advantage of the previously unthinkable economies of scale God will produce, it was announced that beginning on the first of the year, all media currently produced by the separate entities would cease, to be replaced by the following:

(1) *The Magazine*, a weekly collection of celebrity profiles, gossip, fashion, and capsule reviews of new products on offer from The Magazine's advertisers;

(2) *The TV Show*, a 24-hour network featuring celebrity profiles, gossip, true-crime, news with a touch of humor and the paranormal, with sports scores and stock quotes crawling across the bottom of the screen;

(3) *The Newspaper*, a single 8.5 x 11 inch sheet of unrelated facts for today's rich, upscale, young, with-it, beautiful, hip, smart urbanites; and

(4) *The Electronic Thing*, an extremely expensive digital version combining poorly-realized facsimiles all of the most crass elements of all the other old-media products."

The document, bearing over 30 signatures, concluded with: "...Though we are certain that there will be a necessary period of adjustment, as media consumers get to know our new lineup, we are also certain that these products will combine the maximum profits for God, while cutting our production costs to the merest fraction of their current levels. And who cares if you don't like it, anyway?"

Though industry analysts were hesitant to speak on the record, perhaps because of the possibility of being blackballed by "God," privately they expressed concern. "I'm just lucky to have a brother in the plumbing business," said one. "After January, it'll be 'God's way or the highway!'"

The conference, which was televised on all major networks and 50 cable channels, was a masterpiece of pomp, with the Waldorf's already-opulent meeting room sporting 20 foot likenesses of each bigwig. The organizational chart alone was nearly one hundred feet square. To top it off, the chorus of CEOs was accompanied by the entire London Symphony Orchestra, recently acquired by Mr. Murdoch in a poker game. "You ain't seen nothin' yet," said Goldstein. "I designed the company uniforms, and you can see *everything*."

to it with heat. "Since January, I have spent over 100 hours in a state of drug-induced schizophrenia, just to get a sense of what my readers want to see in a magazine. I plan to do as much of that as my schedule will allow."

"It's not our job to tell people what to do or not to do with our products. Frankly, I think that smacks of imperialism, or at least know-it-allism." [See "Marketing to the Ign'ant," page A3.]

As one might imagine, other eager clients are queueing up for Flaw's services. He has just signed a deal to pay NASA $120 million to throw nine tons of Gro-Rite lawn fertilizer out of the space shuttle as it orbits the earth. "Why stop there?" asks Flaw. "I can imagine a day when people will buy stuff, put it on huge rockets, and shoot it into the center of the sun. My job is to make that day come as soon as possible."

"Destroy Your Way to Profits"

BY THE WENDS
Staff Reporter of THE BULL STREET JOURNAL

When Steve Flaw and his boutique ad agency La Grippe were charged by client Pepsi-FritoLay to come up with exciting new ways for customers to use their products, he knew he had to take chances big agencies don't. Think creatively. Break down barriers. He didn't know, however, that his eventual answer could be summed up in these simple words: *throw the products away.*

"It just came to me," says Flaw, grinning at the memory. "One day I was pouring out some milk that had gone bad and gotten all chunky. Suddenly I thought—who says you can't pour milk out before it goes bad?"

Pepsi-FritoLay execs were impressed. "It was beautiful in its simplicity," says Pepsi VP Susan Klum. "Almost a Zen thing, you know? We ordered up a ninety million dollar campaign right away."

The rest is history. The ads debuted during last January's Super Bowl, and depicted a singing, dancing, multiethnic group of attractive teens pouring Pepsi into toilets, down drains, and out the portholes of luxury ocean liners. Within hours sales of Pepsi had gone up seventy percent, and cities nationwide were reporting overloaded sewer systems.

"Pepsi shouldn't care what you do with their products once you've bought them—eat them, drink them, blow them up with high explosives," says Flaw, now regarded as a guru in the new field of consumer product destruction. "And I am the teacher who taught them not to care."

Pepsi immediately recognized that the potential was too great to limit this technique just to its soft drinks, and asked for a campaign for its snack foods. Flaw came up with a series of ads depicting "Baywatch" heartthrobs David Hasselhoff and Pamela Anderson burying cartloads of Fritos in mine shafts, deep below the surface of the earth. Plans are afoot to purchase the Marianas Trench, rename it "The Baste Place," and encourage consumers to buy Pepsi's turkey basting products and send them back

no reason that the mentally-challenged can't consume right alongside the rest of us," Camshaft says. "Hell, it's their right to buy things, whether they want to or not... We didn't fight the Cold War for forty years to just turn around and say, 'You have plenty of disposable income, but I guess you're too *insane* to buy things.' How ridiculous!"

to Pepsi, who will then dump them into the ocean's deepest crevasse.

This craze for destruction has also had unexpected spillover into the so-called third world: villagers in India and Pakistan have been selling their roosters, cows—even children—in order to buy Cool Ranch Doritos. Instead of eating the dearly-bought snacks however, they dump them in their wells, contaminating the ground water with harmful levels of partially hydrogenated soybean oil. Pepsi's Klum disavows responsibility:

"...If They Can Make It There...": Chickutech's Biddies Hit the City

BY HAROLD I. COHAGAN

Special to THE BULL STREET JOURNAL

NEW YORK—Chickutech, a relative fledgling in the poultry industry, has bet the farm on a bold experiment: raising free-range chickens in the mean streets of Manhattan. Speaking from the company's stylish loft in Soho, Chickutech's founder, Brent Biltmore, says that as surprising as it may appear on its face, the move makes good economic sense.

"New Yorkers consume more chicken per capita than any other people in the world. Why," he thought, "don't we spend money on shipping when we can raise the birds right in town?"

Mr. Chicken

Biltmore also noted that free-range chickens, or fowl allowed to roam unrestricted from hatching to maturity, can fetch approximately 25% more in the supermarket than their depressed, less-worldly stay-at-home counterparts. "Our research shows that free-range chickens are less neurotic and unhappy, and that means less harmful fear hormones get released into the meat. Like 'mad cow disease,'" there also appears to be a 'sad chicken disease,' too," said Sandy Grossfeld, Chickutech's head of R&D. "There's a certain type of person who will pay more for what they perceive to be a more wholesome product. Obviously, there are quite a lot of these people in New York—there's quite a lot of every type of person in New York," Biltmore adds, jovially.

Creating a free-range chickenry allows Chickutech to spend a lot less money to raise the poultry. "Can you imagine how much renting a chicken ranch in, say, Greenwich Village would cost? And then there's the issue of hiring all those chicken wranglers," says Biltmore. "This way, all they have to do is check in once a day—a phone call is enough—just to let us know if they're in trouble or have been eaten."

What makes this whole operation possible is that most species have a little-known, but very powerful, homing instinct; this ensures that Chickutech's living inventory doesn't scatter itself to the winds. "We couldn't lose them if we wanted to—there's no changing a chicken's mind once it's made up," says Grossfeld. A couple have even taken the subway to get back to the City before nightfall; evidence suggests that these footloose fowl went to Mystic, Connecticut to see the fine maritime museum there. With a little pride, Biltmore adds, "We don't know how they did it; we're doing some tests, so hopefully all our free-range chickens can take the Metro-North commuter trains, and have even more freedom."

From its founding in Nashville in 1972 until the late 80's, Chickutech raised non-organic chickens. "We used some sort of putty to make them," says Grossfeld. "But then everyone got much more health-conscious and it was organic, organic, organic all the time, twenty-four hours

a day. So we switched to flesh-and-blood. Now free-range is the rage, so that's what we provide." CEO Biltmore echoes this responsiveness to the fickle tastes of the market. "Raising chickens is a little like raising children," says Biltmore. "There comes a time when you have to let go, and hope that the values you've instilled, the lessons you've taught, will keep them out of trouble. And mostly, that's true—there are a few bad apples out there, but they're the minority, believe me."

Only a few months old, Chickutech's master plan still has a few glitches. The company admits that it might be easier to raise free-range poultry in the country. "We've lost a few to traffic. Okay, a lot. Seventy, eighty percent. But the cabs are the worst, and once we educate them, we feel that the mortality rate will be much lower," says Hugo Blunt, head of Chicken Safety for the company. Chickutech is set to distribute a brightly-colored sticker reading "Don't hit that chicken!" free of charge to Manhattan's 2500 cabs. (The sticker is in Arabic, Creole, Farsi, Russian and Tasmanian, as well as English.)

Perhaps more troubling in the long run, is the issue of chickens eating garbage and engaging in other unsavory activities. "Raising chickens with birthday hats on them, then that's what we'd provide. This business is customer-driven; the only opinion we aren't interested in, is the chicken's."

Still, since it began tracking them last April (well before Chickutech came to town), the New York City Police Department has seen the incidence of poultry crimes skyrocket in the five boroughs. Biltmore is unconcerned—even though it is unclear whether or not Chickutech is financially liable for the mayhem its feathered charges cause. "If one of our chickens commits a crime, we kill it. What greater punishment is there?

"Of course, we kill them anyway. But that's besides the point, I think."

For Video Game Lawsuit, It's "Game Over"

BY CHESSIE SCHWARZ

A Staff Reporter of THE BULL STREET JOURNAL

MINNEAPOLIS—After months of having to pee frequently from nervousness, electronic companies in America and abroad breathed a heartfelt sigh of relief today, as a Minnesota District Court struck down an attempt by a disgruntled customer to sue Japanese video game giant Intendo, Inc. Theodoric M. Quimby, 29, of Minneapolis, claimed that playing Intendo games caused him to "lose or otherwise spend ungainfully occupied" nearly a quarter of a million hours of his life.

"This time could have been better used by Mr. Quimby," read the deposition, "who could hardly afford such a handicap (look at him, folks) to further his career. If we can call it that." The document referred to Quimby's self-described 'resumé', which consisted of high scores, levels reached, and 'Princesses rescued.'

"Perhaps he could have become a doctor, like he had planned to, for a few hours between when he solved 'Super Marachi Bros.' and the release of 'Duum'—or at least to make money at a minimum-wage

McJob somewhere. Hell, cadge change at the bus station, *anything*. Just get out of the basement..."

Mr. Quimby, a small, soft man in thick glasses, jerked spasmodically as the verdict was read. Throughout the trial, his intermittent low moan and more frequent cries of "Get 'im!" could be heard, until the defense secured a motion to have Quimby gagged. They felt that the plaintiff was engaging in a sly gambit to win sympathy.

The suit, filed in the Seventh District Court of the State of Minnesota, was for just over million dollars. Mr. Quimby's estimation of the loss of revenue to himself since age seven.

"In 1975, Pong came out," and I was hooked on progressively more and more elaborate, engrossing, and ultimately irresponsible games since then." Quimby had filed earlier suits against Atari, Intellivision (along with its spokesperson, George Plimpton), Coleco Football, Sega, Genesis, Sony Playstation, and Jaguar. These had all been for the same amount as above, except for the action against Coleco, which had only been for $35,000—"because it was lousy, and I

only played it for a few minutes on a trip to Ohio until my Dad got irritated and threw it out the car window."

The judge, Milton K. Wasserman, dismissed the suit on the grounds that Mr. Quimby "was an idiot" and "a loser" and "probably couldn't have gotten a job anyway." Quimby's lawyer, Sonny Shysterino, said that they planned to appeal the ruling. "When you're a lawyer with the last name I have," said Mr. Shysterino, "you're no stranger to adversity. We'll fight it, for Ed and everybody else who's lost their lives to this corrupting pastime."

The suit has become a small cause célebré among members of America's perpetually petulant "Generation X." "We were robbed of our youth by these games," said author Douglas Coplan. "I can't think of any activity more shatteringly worthless than playing a video game, but we all did it. And the sickest among us became proud of it. Instead of preparing for real jobs and careers, we spent all our time chasing blips of light, foxfire. Now, unemployed and unemployable, we're bitter—even Canadians like me."

Q: Can you guess which of these people is a Temporary Temporary?
A: They all are.

These days more and more positions in the labor force are filled by temps. During the Gulf War, Temporary Temporaries provided 23 % of Allied manpower—and 70% of Iraq's feared Republican Guard. The guy who carries the "nuclear football" for the President is a Temp Temp. The person next to you is probably one too. Ask him. *Go ahead.*

Why are we the best? We practice what we preach—we're Temp Temps ourselves. No one works at our office for more than 36 hours, from the mailboy to the CEO him/herself. This ad has been written by 114 different temps from 41 different countries, none of whom ever met.

Experts predict that the first temporary President will be placed by 2010. He *will* be a Temp Temp. And if our Temps are good enough for America, they should be able to meet your needs nicely. Give us a call!

1-888-TEMP-YOU

Temporary Temporaries
Priming the Pump of Chaos!

possible is that most species have a ... least to make money at a minimum-wage $35,000—"because it was lousy, and I ... like me."

THE BULL STREET JOURNAL PRESENTS

MARKETING ON MARS:
MAKING THE GRADE
ON THE RED PLANET

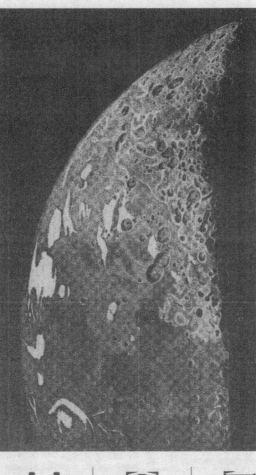

An Executive Conference

Co-Sponsored by
the Chamber of Commerce of Tau Ceti 3
Lunar Cabaña Sheraton
The Moon, U.S.A.

Oxygen Is Limited. Register Today.
For Inquiries and Conference Updates:

F E-mail: conference@BullStreet.com

F URL: http://www.BullStreet.com

The recent discovery of ancient life* on a Martian meteorite has opened the door to opportunities unequaled in the history of commerce on Earth. Through a misguided adherence to hide-bound tradition—or just plain ignorance—businesses in America and abroad have been slow to exploit this new market. This seminar, with a star-studded lineup of speakers, will show you how your company can turn Life on Mars into Money in the Bank!

TENTATIVE SCHEDULE OF EVENTS

Day 1: "The Martian Consumer: A Very Special Breed of Cat"
Day 2: "They Can't Buy It If They Don't Know About It—New Techniques in Intergalactic Advertising"
Day 3: "Not All Neighborhoods Are Alike"—Mini-seminars on marketing to gas giants, cold dead worlds, tiny molten planets (and the corrosive atmosphere you'll find there), planets being torn apart by complex gravitational forces

THESE SPEAKERS MAY/MAY NOT SHOW UP

Steve Jobs, CEO, Next: "Regret? Yes, I Know It Well..."
Nicholas Negroponte, MIT Arrogance Lab: "The Future Will Be As I Say It Will."
Alvin & Heidi Toffler, Fortune Tellers: "No Way, Negroponte! Get A Load of *This*."
Al Gore vs. Rep. Newt Gingrich:: "A Cavalcade of Personal Insults and Mudslinging"
Steve Case, CEO, America Online: "The System Is Unavailable. Try Back in 45 Minutes."
and Gryxx, Hive Leader of Xerrjgh Industries: "To Serve Man."

Sponsored By: **THE BULL STREET JOURNAL**

THE IMPORT $ EXPORT BANK

CHARLES SCHWA
DISCOUNT • BROKERS

THE MART

POSITIONS AVAILABLE

Time Traveler

Growing entrepeneurial concern (est. 1994, 1507, 2212, *etc.*) with business needs **experienced** Time Traveler to go back in time and prevent competitors from being born. Knowledge of the Great Temporal Nexus required.

TTs will report directly to the COO and have a secretary. Own TT equipment (Windows-based) a definite +, but firm will provide if necessary. This office offers great advancement opportunities, but it is definitely NOT an entry-level position. Great pay, benefits, car, medical protection from Time Worms and Temporal Brain Spasms provided. Serious (non-crazy) inquiries only. Please send resume to:

Human Resources Manager
2000 K Street, #1307, Washington, DC, 20002, on July 3, 1992. eoe

CORPORATE SCAPEGOAT NEEDED

Fortune 500 concern based in South needs focus for company-wide need to focus. Basic aspect of human psychology—need to blame all problems on "the Other"—creates OPPORTUNITY for you! Previous officeholders endured tar-and-feathering, burning-in-effigy, elaborate show-trials at stockholder's mtgs, Maoist self-incrimination, more. Experience as "Welsh sin-eater", Jewish son a +! Do you have what it takes: good immune system, quick reflexes, Top 20 MBA? It's the toughest job you'll ever love! Send resume to:

Inhuman Relations
Box 39009
Atlanta, GA 56034

POSITIONS AVAILABLE

SPANKOLOGIST

Major U.S.-based securities firm has an immediate opportunity for this key member of their management team. Individual will have responsibility for both disciplinary and recreational spanking in all of our offices worldwide. Heavy travel. Must be on call to top execs 24/7. Some role playing & costumes likely. Ideal candidate will have 5+ years experience in corporate spanking environment, B.A. with some graduate work. Exceptionally strong communication skills, palms essential. Compensation package commensurate with skills, experience and discretion. Please call, write or fax:

Blake Davison, President
Davison Securities
12 Business Park Way
Dallas, TX 82344
405-555-2332/405-275-2333 fax

We are an equal opportunity employer, but as they say, "some people are more equal than others."

Davison Securities

BUSINESS OPPORTUNITIES

Think that the human race has run out of pristine areas to despoil, virgin lands to exploit, indigenous cultures to destroy?

The Walker Brown Group has literally dozens of unexplored parts of the globe to discover. Our offices can provide you with colonies for that mercantile economic policy, raw materials for a growing Ricardoan industrial sector, or illiterate savage peoples to complete enormous, pointless schemes. In the past five years, we have helped ambitious Civilized Worlders launch:

- the Ultra-Canal, linking the Nile and the Mississippi
- the colonization of the bottom of the ocean floor
- the cutting down of the Amazon rain forest to make room for the world's largest parking lot, with room for 170,000,000 cars
- the war between hurqans and insects
- cancer.

ANNOUNCEMENTS

VICE PRESIDENT SALES

Staffing a new venture? Pointlessly expanding an old one? Our bad luck is your good fortune! Rail accident has left us with a massive overstock of Vice Presidents. Most college educated, some slightly dented/torn labels, all 100% management material! VPs of all sizes and shapes to match any decor. Rock-bottom prices! Send for color booklet.

Executive Staffing Associates
Milford, CT 06447

Men! Women! Have What it Takes to Be A...

TOBACCO INDUSTRY
E X E C U T I V E

Are you a tough-minded, market-savvy, definitely unfiltered college graduate? Industry leader is looking for the next generation of executives as old ones die. Who will usher the cigarette into the 21th Century and beyond? Do you have the nerve, the guts, the b-lls? *We h-pe so!* Experience with class-action litigation a plus. Flexible, rough 'n' ready morality a *definite* plus. Three pack/day preferred but not essential.

Albemarle Tobacco
One Albemarle Way
Albemarle, NC 76578

LEGAL NOTICES

UNITED STATES COURT OF APPEALS
SECOND CIRCUIT

CALLIOPE PRODUCTIONS, INC.,
Plaintiff,

Case No. 96 71283 (JLG)

v.

HARLEQUIN ENTERPRISES, LTD.
Defendant

PLEASE TAKE NOTICE: that the Defendants Harlequin Enterprises, Ltd. ("Harlequin") have initiated a counterclaim against plaintiff Calliope Productions, Inc. ("Calliope") naming Calliope for breach of contract; all entities with possible claim, claim defined as either *** shhh, please, please don't say anything. Don't look up. Just act natural, act like you're just reading a nice, normal, regular legal notice. You've got to help me. I don't know how I got here or what these people are, but they're crazy. They all wear business suits and it looks like a regular office, except there aren't any windows and they implanted this little thing in the roofs of our mouths that starts making this screaming sound if we get more than five feet from our cubicle. I can feel it with my tongue, it's right under my palate. The guy next to me says that the reason there aren't any windows is because we're five miles underground. He says that we are here as Thrall-Servants and that eventually when we wear out, when we can't type anymore, that they take us down to the Stomach Chamber and feed us to the Queen—except the Queen isn't even a person, nobody knows what she is, she might have been a person once or part of her might have been a person, but...wait, someone's coming—claim defined as either: (1) a right to payment, whether or not such right is reduced to judgment, liquidated, unliquidated, fixed, contingent, matured, unmatured, secured or unsecured, or (2) a right to an equitable remedy for breach of performance, upon Calliope, must immediately *** okay, he's gone. All of the Queen's drones, they're the guys in the suits, they all walk in the same rhythm and breathe at the same time—the guy next to me says that they all breathe at the same time that SHE's breathing, that they're all part of the Hive Mind. He says that the drilling noise we can hear is the drones trying to drill a tunnel big enough for them all to attack the surface at once, they'll be done in two months and then everyone on Earth will know the Thrall, that the Queen is laying eggs and soon—what? No sir, nothing, I was just—I know, but...no, please! No! AHHHHHHHHHHHHHHHHHHHHHHH!!!!!!

The Wall Street Journal wishes to apologize for the proceeding breach of decorum. We know that our readers rely on timely, accurate and, above all, appropriate information. We shall strive in future to be more worthy of you and the priceless trust you have placed in us.

In accordance with OSHA regulations, the *Wall Street Journal* does not hold its employees or their dependents in any type of "Thrall."

Nor, obviously, are we ourselves the faithful minions of She Who Beckons With The Left Hand. Any pronouncements to the contrary are legally actionable and will be treated appropriately.]

must immediately file the appropriate and executed proof of claim with

LEGAL NOTICES

UNITED STATES BANKRUPTCY COURT
SOUTHERN DISTRICT OF NEW YORK

In re:
SNOPES FAMILY, INC.,
Case No. 1 (really)

THE BULLSTREET JOURNAL

MONEY'S INTERESTING

World Markets: Botswana's New Stock Market Uncluttered By Business
Page C2.

World Markets: Masons Merge With Illuminati in Friendly Takeover/Enslavement
Page C2.

Mutual Funds: Plan Before You Buy, You Clods

BY R. HENRY WILLIAMS

Stiff Reporter of THE BULL STREET JOURNAL

In Grandpa's day, investing in stocks was the private pastime of the polo-pony set. No more! Now, thanks to mutual funds, any shmoe with a few bucks and a live phone can get in on the party. Mutual funds are a good way to invest in America's economic future, whatever it may turn out to be, and a great reason for you to get the *Wall Street Journal* EVERY DAY.

No other investment can deliver that uncanny mixture of anxiety ("It went up! Should I get out?") and despondency ("I am utterly destitute."), that the stock market is known for. None. Not even "the numbers," and that's not even legal.

But before you take your roll of tarnished pennies to a discount broker, you should have an investment strategy clearly mapped out. (You also should check for "wheats.") This will give you something intelligent to say to Mr. Schwab when he says, "And where do you think you can invest fifty-seven cents?" They hate it when you stare at them like a dope.

Strategy #1: *Read the Business Press*

Reading the business press to uncover "hot" companies and quasi-legit industries with undeveloped potential is perhaps the easiest way to decide which sectors to invest in. Trouble is, can you tell the difference between a legitimate trend and the next hula hoop? Or an authentic hot tip and a story manufactured by some shark-infested PR department, designed to set the stage for some nefarious stock manipulation? Most people can't. Your only hope—and it's slimmer than you re-alize— is to read this paper, and no other, religiously. I can't emphasize that last point enough. About not reading any

other paper. (By the way, *Barron's* is a Commie front Lenin founded it in 1921.)

Strategy #2: *Tried and True Stock Funds*

You're violently risk averse, but for some reason known only to you and God, are investing in stocks rather than good old dirt or gold bars. So you pick a safe bet, with logic somewhat like this: "Everyone needs pins. I'll invest in Thomas Strength Button and Pin Small Cap Fund."

But what about the people who have button and pin phobia (17% of total US population and rising, 1990 Census)? Hah! Bet you never thought of that!

Just because the market is acting strangely, like it has something to hide, or you get the eerie feeling that this has all happened before—in 1929, for starters—don't panic. Don't embarrass yourself by jumping out the window. Instead, ride out the rough parts using a method called "dollar-cost averaging" which means keep pouring money into the Market, no matter how bad it gets. Think about it: if the novice investors all leave at the whiff of a downturn, who will be left to bear the brunt of the losses? That's right, the experienced investor; and we'll be God-damned if we let you come in, make a few quick bucks, and then stick it to us! Where were you when the NYSE was down at 1500? At home sucking your thumb, probably. Get back into this sinking ship, you rats! We *order* you!

Leaving bizarre fears aside for a moment, sometimes a fund can be too safe and mundane. Concord Emerging Foundation Garment hasn't risen a single penny since the introduction of the whalebone corset in 1803. Of course, it was one of the top performing funds throughout the 1700's; "past performance does not guarantee future returns" was never truer than with Concord Emerging Foundation Garment!

It is axiomatic, but bears repeating that there is no room for a romantic when making buy or sell decisions. Just because you had one or two when you were a kid is no reason to put your IRA in Granite Hamster and Gerbil Aggressive Growth. Be strong, do

your homework, and let the gerbils cannibalize each other and dance in their own feces! (As the legendary Jay Gould once said, "Never invest in small animals.")

However, it is important to remember that mutual funds are a gamble—like taking the Bears over the Jets, plus seven—and that even the most prudent investor among us can get skinned. This is called, in the language of the professional money manager, "crapping out."

If you do "crap out," remember that you're not alone. Any mutual fund that plummets, means that we're all *mutually* screwed. Yet another sector of American industry has entered the toilet, never to emerge again. Any catastrophe that sends the markets into freefall— probably a lot of people died, so cheer up, you could have been one of them. Believe it or not, it's better to be poor than dead.

Strategy #3: *Don't...Time...the...Market!*

Novice investors often jump into and out of positions at the first sign of trouble. Or, even worse, they buy or sell because their knee is acting up, or they had that dream about the Beatles again. Omens and premonitions may be good for some decisions (like getting married), but investing is definitely not one of them!

When riding out some bad financial weather, keep in mind that it's not just you, but the entire country that's suddenly broke. If the NYSE was at 60 by the end of the week, we'd all be back in the Stone Age. Misery loves company, so doesn't that make you feel better? Happy investing!

MARKETS DIARY

4/4/97

Stocks

Dow Jones Industrial Average

	Su	M	T	W	Th	F	Sa
100000							
5600							
5500							
5400							
1000							

Day's Activity

Nap Time / End
9 11 1 3

INDEX	Monday	Tuesday	Wednesday	Thursday	Friday
Greed 100	up	up	up	up	up
FearDaq	up	up	up	up	up
Amoralityex	up	up	up	up	up
Panic (Tokyo)	up	up	up	up	up
L'Ennui (Paris)	up	up	up	up	up

BONDAGE
as Practiced by Suburban Couples, 1996

Man- (and woman-) hours per day

Greenwich	
Bethesda	
Winnetka	
Madroma (WA)	

14 12 10 8 6 4

SALES	Monday	Tuesday	Wednesday	Thursday	Friday
Handcuffs	up	up	up	up	up
Eyemasks	up	up	up	up	up
Clamps	up	up	up	up	up
The Cage	up	up	up	up	up
Mustard	--	--	--	--	brisk

OUR INTEREST *in this Parody, Jan-Aug 1996*

Day's Optimism

Nap Time

Jon
Rob

Do Jet Plane Crashes Predict the Market?

By Fatima Happy

Staff Reporter of The Bull Street Journal

If every market close since October 1936 is any guide, it seems that what's good fro the stock market, is bad for air travel—and vice versa, according to a new statistical analysis done by Baltimore mutual fund gurus T. Rowe Price.

The study, leaked to the *Journal* but still officially under wraps by the FAA and SEC, suggests that when the New York Stock Exchange goes up, planes go down. In droves. For every 10 points higher the NYSE closes over the previous day, there is a .00004% greater chance of a major airplane crash occuring somewhere in the contiguous 48 states. It makes you *think*.

"We're still trying to figure out why, but the statistics are pretty convincing," said Sally Gould, an analyst for Price. "Perhaps the pilots get giddy with their profits, forget something important and plow into mountains, trees, hard clouds, et cetera."

"It's really nothing to worry about, even for the heavy business traveller," said William Cotton, a spokesperson for the Federal Aviation Association. "You run a bigger risk in your own bathroom—particular if you shower with a hair dryer, as I do."

The next step is proving the theory is obvious: crashing a few planes on purpose. Price's Gould says: "Of course, we hope that people don't have to be on board, for it to work, but if they do...well, it's all for the good of Science, right?"

Mr. Cotton at the FAA laughed when it was suggested that there were secret plans afoot to intentionally crash selected commuter flights. "Who told you *that?* I'm going to kill you now."

"If a definite link were established, there would be tremendous pressure exerted from the financial community," said an analyst from Bare, Sterns. "Wall Street would be all over the pilots—'Crash it, crash it, we'll pay the families'—so I hope it's just a coincidence."

Schwa Hopes Crime Starts to Pay

New BM 1000 index fund allows anyone to get 'piece of the mayhem'

By Mercy Mi

Staff Reporter of The Bull Street Journal

After riding America's teenager-like crush on mutual funds to dizzying heights of prosperity, discount brokerage Charles Schwa is sure it has discovered the next big thing in investing: the underground economy. Beginning next Wednesday, Schwa plans to offer its ten million customers shares in the Schwa Black Market 1000 no-load fund, the first-ever of its kind.

"The black market is a perfect investment," said Megan Inertia, herself an excon, who will act as manager for the fund. "High returns, international scope, no taxes. It's so flexible; there's always a new way to make money in the underground economy. In 1945, it was cigarettes, chewing gum and fresh eggs. Today, it's low-quality Chinese knock-offs of Microsoft Word.

Did I mention you pay no taxes?"

According to an advance copy of the prospectus provided to the *Journal* , the BM 1000 is an index fund, which attempts to keep pace with the sector as a whole. "Whether it's a huge Colombian drug cartel, or a tiny 'chop shop' on the North Side of Chicago, the BM 1000 will be there... We will manage our assets as aggressively as possible, without pissing the wrong people off and ending up stuffed in some dumpster in Brooklyn with our big 'toe lodged in our throat!'" The prospectus also adds, "Please note that the BM 1000 will be involved in scams, stings, embezzlement, the ol' switcheroo and other activities not practiced by the more genteel portions of society. Though the fund will be managed by Schwa employees, its performance will be determined to a large degree by the effectiveness of law enforcement activities, as well as the dubious morals of hardened criminals. As such, we strongly recommend not 'busting balls,' regardless of the level of returns."

Heloise Pm, head of public relations for Schwa, said that the company first investigated the shadier side of commerce in 1995, somewhat by accident. "Customers were so keen to get into the stock market, that they were coming into our offices with personal belongings—watches, furs, silverware. At first we said no, we only take cash, but then it got too lucrative to pass up. Someone would hock a diamond ring for fifty shares of Neuberger and Berman Guardian."

Within months, Schwa had a network of fences all over the world. It was a simple step into full-fledged malfeasance.

And why not? According to a 1994 report by a team of Stanford economists, the worldwide black market has posted a staggering 23% annualized return since World War Two. "Even if you get rid of a perennial star like the heroin sector," said Charles MacMillan, who tracks the underground economy in his newsletter, *Dirty Money*, "you still have returns of 17-18 percent. Year in, year out, the black market's a great place to put a nest egg."

Schwa hopes that the fund will deliver such high returns that normally law-abiding investors will put aside their morals and invest. "I don't care what religion you are," said Ms. Inertia, "seventeen percent a year makes Treasuries look like flushing your money down the john." Well-greased religious leaders have remained silent on the morality of Schwa's plans. "Does it not say in the Bible, 'See no evil, hear no evil, speak no evil? Well, it says *somewhere*," said Gerry Mander, professor at the Harvard Divinity School. "I think that posting three percent after taxes is a lot more sinful than what Schwa is doing."

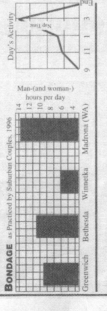

BONDAGE as Practiced by Suburban Couples, 1996

Man-(and woman-) hours per day

Greenwich Bethesda Winnetka Madrona (WA)

Be Glad You Weren't Born Yet in 1929

They called it Black Friday. Some people thought things were awful at the beginning of that horrid week, on Pink Monday. Others thought that surely it was as bad as it could get two days later, on Orange Wednesday. And all agreed that we'd reached the nadir, on Mauve Thursday. Certainly things couldn't get worse—certainly the world couldn't be so cruel.

And yet it could. Thus, that Friday became a day that will live in infamy, as long as men trade, wear neckties, and use the word "infamy."

The weather report on Black Friday was a simple one: "It's raining stockbrokers!" But no umbrella could protect the flappers and bathtub gin-drinkers below from the human deluge. Millionaires became paupers. Paupers became indigent. The indigent became plants. On and on it went.

Hoover had been President for less than a year, but soon his name would be used everywhere to express despair. Encampments of the poor were Hoovervilles. Newspapers were Hoover-blankets. Cantaloupe were Hoover-melons. (No one knows why.) Only yesterday it had been the Roaring Twenties. Now it wasn't, but it was still the Twenties. How could this be? Even professor-types were puzzled.

Confusion reigned.

This, then, was the Great Depression. But why was it so "Great"? Obviously people weren't thinking clearly. Remember, they also called W.W. I the "Great War." Sometimes old people are hard to understand. Take a look at those old newsreels where they walk so fast, you'll see what I mean.

What had brought all this about? A decade of deflationary monetary policies. Utter complacency in both political parties. Wild speculation in high-technology stocks, particularly those having to do with the so-called internet. And, waiting in the wings, a humiliated Great Power.

Thank god that's all behind us.

—*Frank Discussion*

Herbert Hoover, hermaphrodite.

Amish Technologies Stock Soars Over Airbus Deal

By Doug Agrave

Staff Reporter of The Wall Street Journal

Not every tech stock is retreating: the stock price of Amish Technologies (AMT), a fledging aircraft company headquartered in Lancaster County, Pennsylvania has *septupled* in the week since it was awarded a $4 billion contract to design and manufacture the next generation of Airbus medium-haul jets. The award, which stunned the industry, makes tiny Amish not only an equal partner in the prestigious European consortium, but also "the company to beat" in the hyper-competitive world of aircraft design. Now investors are rushing to hitch their buggies to Amish's rising star.

In a letter posted to *The Bull Street Journal*, Amish CEO David Stoltzfus wrote that the contract took the 15-person company somewhat by surprise. "We delivered the proposal, and just two weeks later, we were told. 'O.K., we'll go with thee. Doest thou need any help with thine scale-up?'"

According to Lin Eister, editor of *Plane and Copter*, there has always been a strong undercurrent of aviation in the Amish community. "It was only a question of whether their beliefs would allow it. After the Amish leaders agreed earlier this year that designing, testing and constructing jet airliners would not make them 'conformed to the world' (Romans 12:2), it was only a matter of time."

But not surprisingly, some in Lancaster County are strongly opposed to aircraft-building—"First it is planes, and then it may be something else, and pretty soon thou art chattering away on thine cel phone, stuffing thy face with processed foods and haw-hawing to *Roseanne*," charged a recent editorial in the local paper. But Amish Technologies designer Samuel Stoltzfus wrote, "Our interpretation of the *Ordnung* [the Amish blueprint for expected behavior] allows us to design, test and build jets. Other sects may not agree, and we respect their beliefs. But we also ask their respect for our beliefs."

Please Turn to Page C2, Column 1

What if You Opened a Market and No One Came?

Botswana Bourse is Uncluttered by Business

BY MARSHA LOWLANDS
Staff Reporter of THE BULL STREET JOURNAL

In a silent setback to the capitalization of one of Africa's poorest nations, the opening of Botswana's long-awaited stock market was met with no reaction at all.

On its first day of trading, the Botswana Stock Exchange (BSE) closed at 0, with 0 shares traded in what can only be described as very light activity.

"I'm sorry, I can't talk right now. I'm really upset," said Nelson Ikwana, president of the BSE, wiping tears from his eyes. "It's, like, I sent out invitations, I got food, chips, soda, but..." And then Mr. Ikwana burst out crying and ran from the room. An associate described Mr. Ikwana as "locked in his closet, hugging a teddy bear, listening to Rush's rock opera 2112."

Michael S. Prolix, African desk chief of Salomon Bros. in London, said that the snubbing of the BSE was "certainly nothing personal." He said that all of his traders had previous commitments, and a few were "unable to get to Botswana even if they wanted to." He said that the low prices on the BSE would make it an "irresistable buy, very, very, very soon."

Asked if he was saying this just to avoid hurting the Botswanans' feelings, Mr. Prolix said, "Of course, but don't tell."

"I mean, in the past six months, I had to go to openings of stock markets in Slovakia, Belarus, Turkmenistan, Sudan, and Djibouti," he added. "It got to the point where I was just phoning in trades, not caring where I was, who I was talking to, and whether what I was suggesting was legal or not! Don't tell that, either."

The president of neighboring Namibia, which opened its own stock market last week (up .02 to 3.23, in moderate, almost lackadasical, trading), could not hide his glee at the abject failure of the BSE's first day of, well, business. "We totally planned ours first," said Hon. William Nkrumah. "And when Ikwana said, 'Well, we'll do ours together,' knowing that I had already sent out my invitations and ordered sandwiches and pizza, I told him 'Get bent!' Don't tell that. And he got all puffy and said, 'Fine, so I'll just open my stock market without you and your stupid stock market,' and I said, 'Fine, go right ahead and try,' and so he said 'Fine.'"

His lower lip quivering, Mr. Nkrumah then admitted, "I love that stupid jerk. But don't tell."

Other Market Activity

The Nikkei index moved lower today, falling just over 33 thousand points, on the news that South Korea had put a curse on it. Observers expected steps to be taken overnight to remove the "whammy," which was thought to have something to do with Japan's unwillingness to formally apologize for impressing Korean women into prostitution during the Second World War. The slump has already been dubbed "The Comfort Women Crash of 1996," by the Japanese media. A high-ranking official in Seoul denied any spell-casting on their part, as he furiously poked a wad of Japanese currency with a long, feathered pin.

In other Japanese news, experts believe that the dollar will trade between 105 and 115 yen this year, after reaching an historic low of a used tissue and a piece of old twine in August of 1995.

Continued From Page 17

Many in the aircraft industry do not hide their scorn for the tiny upstart. "They don't use electricity, for God's sake," said an official for Seattle-based Boeing. "What are they going to do, make it out of wood?"

According to the preliminary plans released last week, that is exactly what they plan to do. The 250-seat jet, designed to replace the vast numbers of aging DC-10s in airfleets around the world, will be hewn from oak, and planed to tolerances within 1/2 of an inch. The only decoration on the airframe will be a small beard under the plane's nose. They will then be rubbed with linseed oil to increase their aerodynamics. (It will also give them a pleasant tawny color.)

The jet's lack of jet engines marks a radical departure from contemporary design. Instead of massive turbines or propellers, the Amish plan uses 2,300 pigeons—specially-trained to wing their way back to whatever destination. Airports will thus be required to house huge teams of birds, one full cohort for each city. They will also have to be constructed near cliffs with sheer drops not less than 1,000 feet: "The jet will be laid on the shoulders of 75-100 horses in the cargo bay. These horses will pull the jet at approximately 12 mph at a full gallop, which they must reach before the cliff's edge.

Landings may be bumpier than usual (no rubber tires). But on the other hand, the lack of jet engines on the new jet make the ride quiet as the flutter of 2,300 pigeons."

FAA officials are not thrilled over the Amish design, citing its lack of electricity as "a major concern." But the Amish public relations firm King, Fisher, Beiler and Stoltzfus retained by Amish Technologies deflects this criticism saying, "Why are not candles sufficient for lighting the cabin, as long as proper ventilation is provided? And the technologically-dependent jets are often faulty, with their engines falling off and all things exploding. Birds are not flammable, and our fuselage has no moving parts to fly off. Amish Technologies is putting the craft back in aircraft."

Airline officials are enthusiastic about Airbus' move. Tina Potts of Trans Global says, "People are ready for a flying experience that harkens back to a simpler time."

As the controversy swirls, Amish Technologies prepares to forge ahead—using the influx of cash that the market has provided. "In the Spring and Fall, the demands of the crop preclude any work. Thus, we will have airplane-raisings every Tuesday and Thursday in November. With all the able-bodied menfolk working together, we will fill Airbus' order quite handily." Whatever the outcome, one can be sure the markets will be watching.

Freemasons Seize Illuminati As Secret Society Buyouts Occur In Broad Daylight

BY WILLIAM T. OVERTURE
Special to THE BULL STREET JOURNAL

TWO MILES UNDERGROUND—In a move certain to have repercussions throughout the paranoid realm, the Secret and True Freemasons have announced a hostile takeover of the Bavarian Illuminati.

The Freemasons have offered $74.25 a share for two million "blood places" in the Geneva-based Illuminati, who pioneered the use of the tripped-out "pyramid with that flaming eye with wings" on currency, but have been relatively quiet for the past two hundred years. "Ever since the Rothschilds and the Knights Templar edged us out of the world financial system," says Illuminati spokesman Gnome Chomsky, "we have been exploring new avenues of profits. This unprovoked assault by the Freemasons will be fought most bitterly." He pointed out that after 30 years of inactivity (a well-deserved rest following masterminding the assassinations of Anton Cermak, Dag Hammarskjold, Ngo Dinh Diem, and JFK), since 1990 the Bavarians have moved to take over the world pickle market, have moved aggressively to corner the trade in fez dispensers, and have caused small earthquakes in several Western states.

For their part, Freemason Imperial Hierophant Robert Trump Tower says, "There's a reason the Illumanati are now referred to as the 'Swiss Miss' in our circles—they have been non-competitive for years. We are offering them enslavement with honor." He claimed that the Freemasons will allow most Illuminati to keep their positions, reducing staff and overhead by only ten percent through "attrition, early retirement, and magick."

The Illumati have begun searching for a white knight to save them from the Freemasons. According to Chomsky, overtures have been made to the Rosicrucians, Skull and Bones, the Single-Bullet Theorists, the Trilateralists, and James Angleton's Mole, without any success. "We have, however, had promising leads with Deep Throat and The Druids," added Chomsky.

The proposed takeover of the Illuminati is the largest, but not the first, in the fast-changing, cutthroat market in secret societies. Since the deregulation of paranoia in 1992, this underground industry has followed the lead of banks, airlines, and daily business newspapers in whittling out the little guys. Larger societies can bring considerable economies of scale to their activities, and the middle-sized, "Mom and Pop" cabals just can't compete.

Says industry analyst The Ghost, "It's true that shadow organizations have a long tradition of independence and aversion to profit/loss charts. But this is 1996, and those rules no longer apply." The Ghost added that an infusion of business-school graduates in the last decade has also contributed to the change in methodology. "You can expect to see a real shakeout over the next 18 months, but the brotherhoods which survive will be leaner, meaner, full service cults which can truly meet the needs of their clientele.

"The capture of the Unabomber shows the folly of going it alone in this day and age."

Since 1992, the Posse Comitatus, Roswell Alien Cleanup Crew, and the Cleveland Browns have all been sold, subsumed, or have otherwise vanished without a trace. The Children of Thoth have merged with the Muslim Brotherhood, while the Japanese Yakuza have declared Chapter 11 bankruptcy, claiming skyrocketing insurance premiums and a declining exploitation and fear base, plus an epidemic of Repetitive Motion Disorder from secret handshakes. Even Alger Hiss and Julius and Ethel Rosenberg have been positively identified as dead.

The Ghost added that the explosion in paranoia in the popular media has been the real reason behind the bloodletting. "What with 'The X-Files,' people just don't have any more imagination. It used to be you were afraid of monsters under your bed and gangs of kidnappers in the closet. Now, people pull out their camcorders in order to get them on tape and appear on Oprah."

He also blames the decision of the World Vampire Council to publicly renounce killing the living last February, as a desperate publicity stunt which has further demystified the shadow world.

"What's next?" The Ghost sputters. "Microsoft opening its doors?"

Not all experts are so pessimistic, however. United Nations Secretary General Boutros-Boutros Ghali said that the UN has recently purchased 20 new black helicopters for ferrying Russian troops around the Midwest, and that increased water flouridation in the Third World will create new legions of one-worlder puppets, especially among the desirable 18-49-year-old demographic.

In addition, the explosion of desktop publishing and the Internet has allowed people to start fearsome, far-reaching armies of darkness from their living rooms with an investment of under $500. Dread Robert, who claims a loyal following of 3 around the world, said that he can buy and sell food supplies, publish manifestos, and even vote using his nine-year-old Macintosh SE and a modem. "It's transformed the secret realm. No more initiation fees, paperwork, or skulking. I can keep my day job and move among the creatures of the night, at night."

The mushrooming of do-it-yourself devilry is cold comfort for the Illuminati, who face closing their doors after 500 years, second only in length to the Cult of Osiris. With his voice mixing anger and sadness, Chomsky said, "It's a shame that what we call 'progress' will be responsible for ridding the world of conspiratorial skullduggery and backhanded evildoing. The secret societies of today are like a Disney-fied version of the real thing."

Michael Eisner could not be reached for comment.

GLORIOUS HUNAN HUMAN HUMAN STOCK EXCHANGE

Quotations as of 4 p.m. Changsha Standard Time

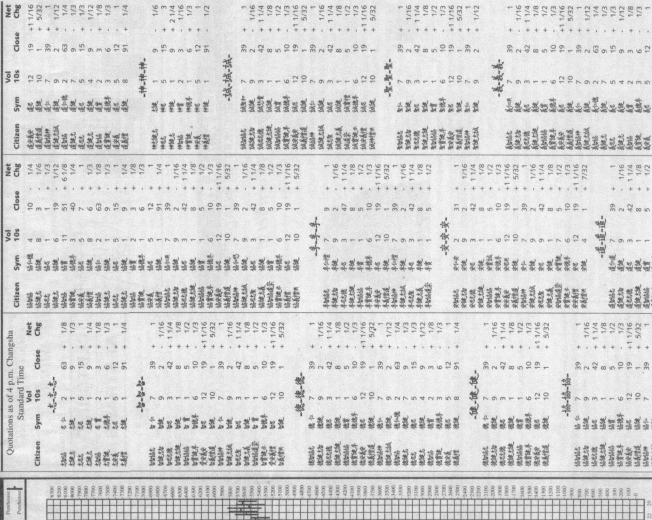

Continued on Next—well, no, not really.

THE DOW JONES AVERAGES

For Entertainment Purposes Only.

Industrials

JOURNAL Jr

A Special Supplement
For Readers 9 to 99!

MARKETING CONTEST

Last week's question, "How would you market this useless invention, an ungainly and ineffective means of locomotion, culled from the scrap heap of The Age of Invention?" was correctly answered by Brian Sappho of Craine, New Jersey. Brian wrote, "First, I would set aside some funds to settle out-of-court with all of the people who would doubtless injure themselves while operating this irresponsible contraption. Then, I would buy a bunch of time on local cable channels, late at night when it's cheapest. Then, I would hire some out-of-work porn stars to parade around in bathing suits and be filmed standing next to—not riding—the invention, which I would call "The Ceridwean." Soon, it would be America's latest health craze, and all I would have to do is sit back and count the cash. PS—My dad helped me with this."

So does everybody's, Brian—but you get extra points for being honest! Since you're this week's winner, you and your Dad will receive a year's subscription to *The Bull Street Journal!*

This week's contest is, in our opinion, a little bit harder. It is taken from an engraving of Lord Byron's famous swim across the Dardenelles. Oh, Mr. Big Shot Poet, Mr. Big Swimmer, didn't anybody he was using a contraption! (By the way, the name "The Byronator" is already taken.)

Ask the Mystery CEO

This week's Mystery Chief Executive Officer is employed by the General Motors Corporation. He lives with his commonlaw wife, Veronica, and their two commonlaw dogs, Profit and Loss, in Grosse Pointe, Michigan.

"When I was a youngster, I wanted to be a poet. I hated cars and getting dirty. My father tried to convince me to be a soldier, and when that didn't work, a fightin' poet like Lord Byron. But I wasn't interested in guns, killing, incest, or swimming. My parents even sent me for shock treatments, but they didn't "take." I mean, they influenced my future career in many ways, but I still wanted to be a poet.

Mystery Man

So I used to spend a lot of time indoors, helping my mother with the cleaning, and turning the Romantics into Modernist gobbledygook using my Ezra Pound Encoder Ring. You had to send away to Italy for it. When that package came, it was the happiest day I could remember.

But then, one crisp fall afternoon, I saw my older brother Jake get hit by a car as he played touch football in our street. The car that hit him was a Chevy. That day, as I cradled my brother—who I suddenly liked a lot more than ever before—I swore that I wouldn't rest until Chevy was as dead as Jake was.

To save time, I abandoned poetry and devoted the next three decades to working in the automotive industry. After hard work and some truly masterful backstabbing, I became CEO of General Motors. Needless to say, I am plotting even as we speak to drive a stake into this company's foul heart. Because *they made the car that killed my brother.* Maybe I shouldn't have told you all that. Anyway, don't be shy with the questions, kids. I have some of my own. Questions, I mean. No kids. (My wife repulses me.)

Dear Mr. ?—
I'm sad and mad. I don't like any of my books anymore because they are boring. Plus the dog chewed them. And I can't draw ANYTHING because my hand makes all sorts of crazy lines when I want it to do straight ones. I am so MAD.
Mom and Dad are working and not around to answer my questions. I don't blame them, because "things are not free-of-charge" but I do feel very lonely. My question is, is there Heaven and Hell, and how do you find out which one you're going to? Sorry—Jay McMillan, Little Rock, AR

Well, I'm no priest, Jay—don't even go to Church—but I will tell you one thing: having armies of people frightened of you, who do whatever you say, and having enough money to buy anything you want (even a kayak, if this is what your enclosed drawing is meant to represent), is about as close to Heaven as I can imagine. And that's my life in a nutshell! So, my advice is: forget about drawing and books, they're for stooges. Like poetry! (Read the introduction.) Work insane hours, avoid thinking about anything, and maybe you'll be a CEO like me someday! But probably not.

Dear Mr. ?—
George Washington grew hemp. What do you think of that?—Mycroft Grant, Portland OR

So do I—what do you think of *that?*
Honestly, I think it's great! As a matter of fact, GM is taking the lead in integrating hemp and hemp products into its vehicles. Out of the big three, only our GM cars meet the 2002 California Hemp Standards *today!* All of the filling in our seat cushions is pure Mexican hemp; we also use it in our airbags. (Though I hope you never get to find out, Mycroft!)

But that's not all: some 1998 models are even sporting trim and mouldings made from a hemp-based polymer. And of course our upholstery and interior is loaded with hemp, as it has been since the 1960's. (Looking back, that's one of the few things the so-called "counter-culture" got right!)

Now that you've got me started and my handler won't be back for several minutes yet, I'll let you in on a little secret: our new concept car, the Nebula, is over 87% hemp/hemp products/hemp manufacture leavings. That's everything from the steering column, to the wheelrims, to the engine! As soon as we get our employees to stop stealing portions to take home and smoke, we think we'll have a real winner! *Fortunate Magazine* calls me the "the Cheech *and* Chong of the auto industry," but they'll be singing a different tune when we've locked up the 18-35 market.

Mindful that the real market growth is happening in the countries of Asia and the Pacific Rim, we are currently gearing up to produce a prototype of a car produced completely out of opium. We think that it is the product that will take GM into the 21st Century...and beyond!

Thanks for your questions, kids—time for my medication and "walkies." It's been fun, and I am reassured that America's economic future is in good hands!

Who will be next week's Mystery CEO? Be sure to read *Journal Jr.* to find out! Questions for the CEO should be sent to: Mystery CEO, Post Office Box 2484, Times Square Station, New York, NY 10108. Please include a telephone number and a crude homemade release form.

made the car that killed my brother.
Maybe I shouldn't have told you all

vehicles. Out of the big three, only our
GM cars can meet the 2002 California Hemp

ber and a crude homemade release form.

If Today Is Your Birthday…

You are strong with Pluto, lord of the underworld. But while many people see this — and you — as evil and rapacious, death is a sign of change, of the natural progression of all things in the universe. Therefore, do not let the well-meaning but ignorant dissuade you from keeping to the role which life has assigned. If it means going through with that dismembering of a long-established company or suing your wife, be strong! Also, you are forceful and have a powerful presence, though bright sun does make your eyes burn. The other sex will find you especially attractive in the next year; try to get them to take a bite of the pomegranate, or go in on a time share in the Cayman Islands. Other famous financial figures with your birthday: Milton Friedman, William Walker, Cardinal Richelieu, and John Stuart Mill.

Sagittarius
Mars, the God of War, is in your house, which augurs success in hostile takeovers and mass firings. But beware Venus, in the guise of an artistically-inclined but financially immature paramour, who will cast her spell on you later this month!

Capricorn
Like the stubborn goat, keep butting away at that annoying client; they are closer to buying those 40,000 shares than you think! Also, some T-bills you buy today will come due in 30 days.

Aquarius
The Water Bearer is usually depicted spilling H2O over fertile ground; for you, it means not being stingy with your financial advice at a crucial board meeting. Others are thirsty for your insight!

Pisces
Saturn and Mercury are in perfect conjunction, which has only occurred twice since the creation of the Federal Reserve; both times were met by a huge cut in the basic lending rate. Also, a good time to discuss cattle futures with a Virgo.

Aries
Your sign is a ram, and like a ram, you must keep battering against the iron walls of corporate bureaucracy. A Taurus and a Libra are writing a memo which casts you in an unflattering light.

Taurus
The greatest of earth signs is telling you to keep your investments on the ground today. A cautious investment — T-bills or money markets — will reap great benefits in April or May. Avoid water, as in rain, or showers!

Gemini
Like twins facing opposite directions in the same womb, unemployment and inflation figures will be released today. Read them carefully and look for new connections!

Cancer
Your heavenly bodies are the sun—representing the London and New York exchanges—and the moon—which shines here when the Nikkei is open for business. Keep watch over all of them. Look for an Aquarian ordering food from the local deli, and get in on it, no matter the consequences.

Leo
Stay away from the human resources department: they mean you ill will. Housing starts are released tomorrow, and you should examine carefully any figures which start with the numbers 732. Also, Neptune is ascendant, so avoid junk bonds.

Virgo
The virgin is telling you to go after virgin natural resources, like timber, water, or molybdenum rights. Put aside a breach of contract lawsuit you are currently pursuing with a Pisces.

Libra
Check your Quotron often for a sign that fortune is smiling on you, and then act quickly. Avoid foreigners and Sagittarians, especially those who seem to smile a little too much, if you know what I mean.

Scorpio
Jupiter, king of the planets, enters your house today, brining with it mastery over all things and people, especially agents of the Securities and Exchange Commission. Do not be afraid to make some bold decisions, just like ballsy, headstrong Jupiter.

JUMBLE!

○ ○ __ __ __ __
      O   X   Y

○ ○ __ __ __ __ __ __ __ __
      E   N

__ __ __ __ __ __
N A S D   Q

"__ __ __ __ __ __ __ — 15th makes many a man want
to slit his wrists."

CROSSWORD

CLUE: *"If you pay peanuts, you get monkeys."*

ACROSS
1. Governmental nuisance created by Sixteenth Amendment.
2. Not a kickback, but a…
3. "Pleasure doing business with you, sucker."
4. Frequent sign of midlife crisis.
5. Quasi-legal place to keep your money safe from Feds.
6. Surefire presentation-ruiner (not food-poisoning).
7. First—and last—*Fortune* magazine centerfold, 1967.
8. Robert Rubin's dog.
9. "Gee, boss, that's a nice tie!"
10. Disease acquired in business school.
11. Prep school nickname of host of PBS' *Wall Street Week.*
12. Tax-cut welshing Prez.
13. What OSHA *really* stands for.

DOWN
1. "The business of America is none of your…" Coolidge quote.
2. *The Management Techniques of* _____ *Stalin*
3. What never to say to a Japanese businessman.
4. I see Paris, I see France, I see Mickey Cantor's _____.
5. Price one bank charges another for rolls of pennies.
6. Worst-performing mutual fund in history.
7. Gin-and-_____ (commuter's friend)
8. Founder of the Elks Club and the Ku Klux Klan.
9. He used frequent-flyer miles to reduce his jail time.
10. No brown shoes with a _____ suit!
11. Common dirty joke hidden in spreadsheets.
12. #1 maker of naugahyde briefcases.
13. "Will work for _____"

Stocks: Feline Stock Whiz Still Confounding Experts, Self. *Page A1.*

Review: The New $100 Bill is "an onslaught of Bad Taste." *Page C1.*

Who's News: Microsoft to Launch Lousy New Theme Park. *Page B2.*

Aircraft: Amish Technologies Shocks Industry By Snagging Airbus Contract. *Page C1.*

THE BULLSTREET JOURNAL

THE ANSWER KEY

Random Thoughts, Favorite Jokes and Unsettling Snippets of Reality

For more information about the factual material contained in this parody, and referred to below, for God's sake don't take our word for it—consult your local library.

Page A1: *Clinton Street Luge*
Caffe Roma was (is) a coffeehouse in the basement of Mike's old apartment building in Seattle. For over 300 years, coffeehouses have been breeding grounds for seditious activities, and this one was no exception, if you consider endless rounds of gin rummy seditious. But no matter how politically rowdy the patrons get, you can't hold it against them: they probably drank too much Colombian Supremo Grande Extremo or something, had a lot of excess energy energy energy and didn't know whether to pull down the government or run around in tight circles until the buzz wore off. Roma was (is?) frequented by friendly persons of uncertain employment—like us. And unwilling devotees of the soy milk latté, like Mike.

Page A1: *What's New: Markets*
We're convinced that if they ran out of gin in the Club car of the Metro-North, America's financial markets would grind to a halt the next day; making up for lost time once you get home gives you less

Page A3: *Good for o Foreign Cos.*
When Mike temped at Microsoft (see below), he got lost every morning, because Building 26 looked exactly like every other building on the Campus—thank God it was the laid-back West Coast and they didn't give his back one stripe per minute late or something. Microsoft's Campus, if you've never been there, looks like a particularly prosperous community-college; if they had heads on stakes, Mike didn't see them. That doesn't mean they don't have them.

Page A3: *Journal Editor Noam Chomsky*
"Once I got a look at their 401(k) plan, I realized that all that whining about politics was just the Mother of All Sour Grapes. East Timor, schmeast Timor—we're talking real bucks, here!"

Page A4: *God's Salesman*
Jon just learned that "Tao" is pronounced "Dow" as in Tao Jones Industrial Average. Until he was twenty-one he thought that "frustrate" was pronounced without the first r, that is, "fustrate." Jon worries that he doesn't pronounce any words correctly, but people are too polite to tell him.

Page A6: *We're Running This Article Every Friday*
We have in our possession two computer-enhanced photographs which show a young Hillary Clinton in Dealey Plaza on November 22, 1963. While there is no conclusive evidence she was involved in the assassination, paraffin tests showed that she *did* fire a gun that day.

All jokes about Chelsea Clinton are tongue-in-cheek. Being a teenager is hard enough without some right-wing bozos reading into the *Congressional Record* that you "have a humongous zit on [your] nose."

Page A7: *Letters: Laffer Curve*
The Laffer Curve was supposedly first promulgated with a diagram hastily drawn on a napkin. It's an old saying, but it still bears repeating: "Beware of politicos bearing napkins." Nothing very important, including economic theory, can be explained on a napkin—and we're not just saying that because we're intellectuals.

Page A7: *Dear Mr. President Ad*
Who actually did say "If not us, who? If not now, when?" Please drop us a note at bullstreet.com.

If you want to look smart by quot-

Texas. Just another example of that peculiarly American refrain: they made me take it, but I do remember a few swear words.

Page B3: *Barter Makes a Comeback*
One of the most unsettling things about growing up, especially if you're from the sheltering somnolent suburbs, is realizing that *everything* is negotiable. It's like the world is one enormous souk. The currency of Bhutan, a small country to the northeast of India, really is the Dzongkha.

Someone once told us that every WaWa he's ever gone into has employed at least one balding woman. Perhaps it's leaky microwaves.

Page B4: *Dirt a/k/a soil*
If you enjoyed this article, drop a line to Bullstreet.com for a copy of "The 100 Jesus Chain Letter." It's even harder to understand, and we're more troubling to the thoughtful. (Not recommended for readers under nine.)

Page B4: *Lovecraft's Viscous Villians*
After a adolescence chock full of H.P. Lovecraft (blame Dungeons and Dragons, not faulty parenting), it was a real comedown to finally

are visible to the unaided eye. We've seen the best minds of our generation destroyed by pointless busywork…But those Gen Xers sure can make a paper clip chain!

Page B6: *Video Game Lawsuit*
Things haven't been the same since "Yar's Revenge" (1981). A 12-step group for addicts meets every Thursday night in the Episcopal Church on Madison Avenue. They're tough-lovers, all right—they won't even let you wear a digital watch.

Page B7: *Calliope Legal Notice*
What if aliens really are abducting people? What if aliens are performing bizarre operations on human beings — removing eggs from women's ovaries with knitting needle-type instruments, creating a "communion" between their race and ours? Will they cut any special deals with collaborators willing to sell out the human race? We need to know this before making plans for the future.

Whitley Strieber's agent must be an alien, to be able to sell the same book over and over. Can anyone get us his/her/its number? We're itching to sell the interstellar rights to this thing.

The "schwa" is that strange upside down "e" that dictionaries use to designate a short vowel sound. Any vowel can make the schwa sound — a, e, i, o, u, in certain usual cases even y. The Schwa: masterpiece of pronunciational egalitarianism.

Page C1: *Tapeworm*
Robert Rubin, whatever else you might say about him, has GREAT hair. Thick, fluffy, a nice mix of salt and pepper. Maybe he uses some type of extremely expensive haircare products not available to the average citizen. Alan Greenspan, on the other hand, is actually much more important but has less personal style. He clearly traded his hair for raw power, in the classic Faustian bargain.

Page C2: *Botswana Bourse*
"Bourse" is a great word. "Let's go to the BOURSE!" "See you at the BOURSE!" "You have the most beautiful BOURSE I've ever seen." Maybe you should also be able to use it as a verb: "I'll BOURSE you every which way to Sunday."

Page C2: *Freemasons…*
Opinions differ as to who actually wrote this parody. Some say the Mafia, others finger the CIA, still others a group of disgruntled anti-

Page C1: *Markets Diary*

next day, making up for lost time once you get home gives you less time to recover. And no matter how much disinfectant they use, the bathrooms always smell faintly of juniper berries and vomit.

Page A1: What's New?: Newspaper Editors
What exactly *does* it mean when somebody speaks "on deep background" to a reporter? Do they have to wear some type of disguise? We always envision them whispering hoarsely over the phone, or standing in the murky shadows of a Washington garage, like Hal Holbrook in "All the President's Men."

Page A1: Washington Wire: Backrubs
"Kumbaya" is a corruption of "come by here": i.e., "come by here," "come by here." One of our roommates, a black guy, once remarked incredulously, "Man, you white folks sure love that song." In defense of the musical taste of all white Americans, we reminded him that every pre-school from 1968-1975 sang it on Music Day. Repeatedly. Until the kids were ready to riot.

Page A3: Chinese Stock Market
Though our crime-ing is going down, America *was* mean to Martin Luther King—particularly that bastion of institutionalized meanness, Hoover's FBI. MLK ignored their not-so-polite 1964 suggestion that he kill himself, a real masterpiece of ineptitude: imagine a guy in a white shirt and tie, with really short hair, sitting at a typewriter all day, puzzling over which misspellings sounded most authentic—that's your tax dollars at work, folks. King even showed a pretty good sense of humor about the wiretaps. How different history might have been, if SNCC had a few photos of J. Edgar in his Maidenform bra…

Also, Matthew 5:16 actually says, "Let your light so shine before men, that they will glorify your Father which is in heaven." Where does the Bible say that thing about rich men and heaven? We don't know. Maybe the Bible never says it at all. Remember, Mark Twain never said that thing about frogs and politicians.

Page A5: Ozymandias University MBA Ad
The first reader to correctly identify this location wins US$50. (Yale students, alumni, faculty, staff and their dependents are ineligible for this contest.)

Page A6: The Liberal Media Versus "The Force"
The newly-released version of *Empire Strikes Back* shows Yoda wearing a button saying "Ask Me About 'The Force.'"

Page A6: Aside
Alexander Hamilton, first Secretary of the Treasury and star of the twenty dollar bill, really *did* want the Senate to be hereditary. Some people wanted George Washington to be crowned king. There was a conspiracy in 1934 to overthrow Roosevelt and install a fascist dictatorship. Richard Nixon and George Bush just "happened" to be in Dallas on November 22, 1963. Young people: American history is not as boring as it at first appears—they *have* to teach it that way because the government forces them to.

Page A6: Washington, Wigs and Oats
Every review of a recent biography of George Washington mentioned his powerful, well-developed thighs. It was like you had somehow stumbled upon *Jean Genét's Illustrated Guide to American History*.

If you want to look smart by quoting something (people do this a lot in certain circles) but can't remember who said it, it always works to attribute it to either Thomas Jefferson, A.J. Liebling, or Gandhi. Alternatively, just make up anything and attribute it to one of them. "In the land of the deaf, the one-eared man is king." —M. Gandhi.

Page A7: Salt 'n' Pepa
It should be emphasized that Salt 'n' Pepa would be nothing without their DJ, Spinderella. Someone we know saw them in an elevator and says they're all under five feet tall.

Of course, we must admit that we would be nothing without our DJ, Louis Rukeyser.

Page B1: Once-Booming Cadaver Market
As anyone who works in a morgue would tell you, dead bodies have a disconcerting habit of abruptly sitting up on the coroner's table. It's a natural contraction of the body's ligaments and tendons as a result of rigor mortis. Yet more evidence that the real world is creepy, creepy, creepy. A mortician acquaintence once let us in on a little trade secret: "If you ever get grossed out, think of dollar signs." Good advice for any career.

Page B1: Spider Discovery
The real bonanza would be sunglasses. Think of it, eight eyes each! (They'd be tiny, but I bet the Germans could make them.)

Page B2: Brush With Death
"Il Cornuto," meaning "the cuckolded [one]" is a heaviest-of-duty Italian insult, also expressed in the phrase "wearing the horns", as well as a variation on the "Hook 'Em Horns" hand signal favored by students at the University of

Page C1: Markets Diary
A stockbroker Mike lived with once told him, "The Market is half economics, half psychology." Yikes! Bad claims in the NYSE cafeteria could plunge the world into a second Great Depression. Or running out of gin, for that matter. It's sobering.

Page C1: Dow Diary
On a somewhat related note: why is it that, although nothing important changed in the real world between October 29th and October 30th, 1929, everyone suddenly had to be poor for ten years? Just wondering.

it was a real comedown to finally visit New England and find it wasn't like that at all. Except for parts of Bridgeport, Connecticut.

Page B4: Prison Labor
According to the *New York Times*, Microsoft uses prison labor to pack its software. So the next time you're installing Windows 95, remember that it's probably crawling with serial killer cooties.

Page B4: When Life Gave Them Aliens
This article germinated from being told that abductions tend to run in families and cluster in certain geographic areas. Man, I bet that issue of *Money* would fly off the newsstands—"America's 100 Alieniest Cities."

Page B5: Destroy Your Way to Profits
"La Grippe" is French for pneumonia, or the flu. "Choufleur" is French for cabbage, and is a term of endearment. "Frottage" is…uh, forget it.

Page B5: Magazine for the Insane
Do Interpol agents speak Esperanto? How about secretaries at the U.N.? A few Esperanto sentences to whet your appetite: "La muso amas la hundon." ("The mouse loves the dog.") "Granda planta mangxis la muson." (A large planta ate the mouse.) "La mola krajono skribis noton." (The soft pencil wrote a note.)

Page B6: Free-Range Chickens
Chickutech's chickens are only in New York City from September to June; in July and August, they're out in the Hamptons. (You should see the jitney after they're done with it.)

Page B6: Temp temps
If you look closely, immense lakes of bitterness and regret in this joke

Mafia, others finger the CIA, still others a group of disgruntled anti-Castro Cubans. All had the motive, the opportunity, and the ability—although if the Cubans were involved, one would expect large portions to be written in Spanish.

One thing is certain, however: it is clear that *The Bull Street Journal* could not have been the work of a "lone nut." It is also clear that the three men believed to be its authors—commonly referred to as "the three tramps," were just what they purported to be: PATSIES.

How many of the following ring a bell? The grassy knoll, the Trilateral Commission, Operation Paperclip, the Nugan Hand Bank, MK-ULTRA, Majestic-12, the "Mighty Wulitzer," the P2 Lodge, Danny Casolaro, Felix Rodriguez, Rex-84, Manny Pena, the National Election Service, Smedley Butler, "Raoul," Joseph Holsinger, Ari Ben-Menashe, "east wind, rain," the Order of Perfectibilists, the Gemstone File, Dr. Donald MacArthur, Carroll Quigley, and Mae Brussell. If you became mystified about halfway through, good. Stop now. If you were still nodding your head at the end, it is already too late.

Page C2: Mutual Fund Table
See "New Chinese Stock Market," A3.

Page C3: Contraption
How in the world was that quasi-unicycle thing supposed to work? Was the wheel so heavy that it balanced out the weight of the person? Did you have to change wheels when someone who weighed more or less got on? So what happened when you stopped? You would think these would be questions the inventor would have thought about before starting in the first place. People—ya gotta love 'em. Or maybe not. But at least *try*.

Herbert Hoover, as the book *Hail to the Chiefs* says, "led a very exciting life, but the excitement just sort of rolled off of him and he stayed boring underneath." Hoover once translated *De Re Metallica*, a classic trove of Roman mining information, from Latin into English. And he was an engineer, just like Jimmy Carter. There's a lot more where this came from, if for some inconceivable reason you want it. Also, was that way he combed his hair, from the middle out to both sides, unfortunate or what?

Page C1: Amish Technologies
In the process of researching this article, we found that the Amish have their own WWW page. No kidding.

The real question about the Amish has always been, why choose 1880 as the year when time stopped? Why not 1949, so that you could watch TV, even if your screen couldn't be more than two inches wide? Or 1956, so that you could have a personal computer, even if it cost $90 million and was so large it had to be kept in a barn?

Page C1: Schwa Hopes Crimes…

NOTES FROM A SMALL PLANET

Leading the world around by the nose • By Rick Geary

THE SECRET OF SAILOR NED

RICK GEARY ©21

I HAD JUST ABOUT GIVEN UP ON FINDING THE RIGHT GIRL...

WHEN I CAME ACROSS A MOST COMPELLING AD.

THE ORIGINAL SAILOR NED WAS LEGENDARY FOR HIS POWER OVER WOMEN.

WHEN HE BECKONED THEY LEAPED TO OBEY. SOME EVEN DIED FOR HIS FAVOR.

A NEW COLOGNE HAS CAPTURED THE ESSENSE OF SAILOR NED.

HOW COULD I HELP BUT ORDER A BOTTLE (SATISFACTION GUARANTEED)?

MY NEW AND MYSTERIOUS AROMA APPEARS TO FASCINATE THE LADIES...

ALSO MEN AND YOUNG CHILDREN...

AND ALL THE PETS OF THE NEIGHBORHOOD.

CONTINENTS MOVE BENEATH MY FEET. ENTIRE ECOSYSTEMS TRAIL IN MY WAKE.

NO MORE LONELY NIGHTS.

B

ROZ'S MARVELOUS COLLAGES

Japanese matchbox covers from anonymous artists, 1920-1940 • By Roz Chast

B

WHAT AM I DOING HERE?

Twenty-seven hundred years of a bad idea • By Mike Reiss

Like the Olympics…On Steroids!

I was at the 2008 Beijing Olympics, sitting in Beijing National Stadium. Remember this building? It looks like a giant metal bird's nest. It holds 80,000 people. Or one giant robot vulture.

The 500 million dollar structure was built to last 100 years, but since the Olympics it's only been used a handful of times: a winter carnival, a few pop concerts. It can withstand an 8.0 earthquake but not massive public disinterest.

Not far away is the aquatic center where Michael Phelps won eight gold medals in swimming. This building looks like a huge kitchen sponge that changes colors. It's like something out of a cartoon: Sponge Bob eats a tainted Krabby Patty, and falls on his back, changing hue every few seconds.

It symbolizes everything I love about the Olympics: it's big and colorful and pointless and goofy. Every two years, cities across the world fight for the honor of hosting an event that will bankrupt them. Not only do the Olympics lose money, they leave towns stuck with expensive facilities nobody uses, like a velodrome. If you don't know what a velodrome is, that proves my point.

The locals don't want the games—I lived in Los Angeles during the 1984

MIKE REISS is Intrepid Traveler for *The American Bystander*.

What kind of diarrhea did I get at the Rio Olympics?

Olympics and the entire city cleared out. It was the perfect LA—lots of palm trees, no people. So I bought the cheapest Olympic ticket I could find: a boxing match between Egypt and Cameroon. The two fighters had clearly never seen a fight before. One guy huddled in a corner trying not to get hurt; the other guy rocked from side to side in giant swaying arcs. I've never been in a fight in my life, but I had a sense I could whip both these guys at the same time.

I went to the London Olympics in 2012, and that bustling city hasn't been so empty since the Blitz. Even so, I couldn't get tickets to the Opening Ceremony; I watched the ceremony in a hotel suite, surrounded by former Olympic athletes. They couldn't get tickets either, because if you don't win a medal, you don't get squat. Each year 6,000 Olympic competitors get shafted.

On TV, I watched Sebastian Coe open the Games. Coe won four Olympic medals for running real far, real fast. For that, he was elected to Parliament and was made a Lord; tonight he was addressing a TV audience of 3.5 billion—half the people on earth.

Sitting next to me in that dingy hotel room was the runner Sebastian Coe beat by four seconds. He's now a gym teacher in Connecticut.

Even if you win, that's no guarantee of anything. Sure, George Foreman, Muhammad Ali, and Joe Frazier went from the Olympics to long, lucrative careers beating each other up. Mary Lou Retton morphed from Olympic gymnast to a beloved Broadway Peter Pan. General George S. Patton competed in the 1912 Olympics in pistol shooting; he came in twenty-first. Patton would go on to become one of the least beloved Peter Pans in history.

And what about Primos Kozmus? No, he's not the bad guy in the Transformers movies; Primos Kozmus is the guy I saw that night in Beijing's Bird's Nest Stadium—he won Slovenia's first medal in the hammer throw. He spent his whole life—ignoring his studies, sacrificing his love life—to become the world's greatest hammer throwerer-er. Now that he won the gold medal, what could he do? Work at Home Depot?

Why had I even seen the hammer throw? Because tickets were ten bucks. It costs a fortune to see Pairs Figure Skating tickets at the Winter Olympics; but it's easy to get into the rehearsal. Same skaters, same routines, but many numbers end with the couples screaming at each other. On the ice, in front of everyone. That's what I go to the Olympics for.

You see, I'm not really a sports fan. So I go to the events no one else is interested in: trampoline; race walking; roller hockey. I'm only sad that I missed the old Olympic Sports that were phased out: hot-air ballooning; club swinging;

live pigeon shooting. Everyone remembers Jesse Owens, but what about Charles Downing Lay, who won the gold for America that year in…Town Planning. Town Planning was an Olympic event!

No matter how obscure the sport, you get caught up in it; within ten minutes, you consider yourself an expert. "Nice step rhythm!" I heckled the javelin thrower. "You throw like women's javelin world record holder Barbora Sportakova!" My wife jostled me. "Maybe you shouldn't antagonize the man with the pointy stick and the deadly aim."

Yes, I embody another fundamental aspect of the Olympics: bad sportsmanship. A Russian athlete once told me, "I want English or U.S. referees—they are the only honest ones. Even better is a Russian referee, because they cheat, but for me."

The Games take me all over the globe, and they're generally a reflection of the city hosting them. The 1984 LA Olympics, for example, were a showbizzy affair: they opened with a speech by movie star-turned-president Ronald Reagan. They closed with the arrival of a fake UFO dubbed "the Flying Taco."

At the other end of the spectrum was Pyeongchang, the tiny onion-growing town that hosted the 2018 Winter Games. I asked a local taxi driver to take me to the Olympic Park.

He gave me a blank stare.

I said, "It's the Olympics! It's the only thing in this town!" Blank stare.

I showed him a brochure for the Olympics. It had a map. Olympic Park was written in Korean. None of this got through.

I exploded. "Look, there! That big complex of sports arenas! With a blimp floating over it! I'm pointing right at it! Follow my finger!"

I wound up walking to the Olympics. It was two miles in freezing weather and high winds; when I arrived, I found out many of my events had been canceled due to freezing weather and high winds. They promised me a full refund. It's been three years and I'm still waiting.

The best-run games I ever attended were the 2014 Sochi Winter Olympics. If you remember them at all, it was for the lousy coverage they got in American media: Sochi was a tropical resort, all the snow was melting, and the town was overrun with stray dogs. What a load of borscht—Sochi was plenty cold, much cooler than the seventy degree weather at Vancouver's Winter Olympics. And I only saw two stray dogs in the weeks I spent there. Security at Sochi seemed tight—there were metal detectors everywhere, but not one of them was plugged in.

It was a new Russia—the people were cheerful, helpful and friendly. Clearly, the order had been given to be nice to tourists, because the moment the Olympics ended, the entire nation went back to being surly, sad and drunk.

I remember attending the Opening Ceremony, sitting directly across the arena from Vladimir Putin. My tickets were $1800; I assume he got some discount.

As the magnificent spectacle unfurled, I watched Putin—what was he thinking? Was he proud? Relieved? Bored? Wondering if he could get a refund?

Turns out, what he was thinking was, "In three weeks, I'm invading the Ukraine." **B**

Just When You Thought It Was Safe To Go Outside...

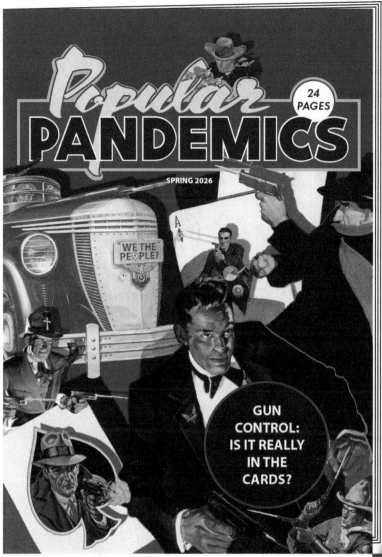

You Discover *Popular Pandemics!*

A hilarious look at our dystopian future through the eyes of our past.

"*Popular Pandemics* is a wonder to behold. I've rarely encountered anything so densely packed with jokes."
—*Stephen Colbert*

"Wow. One person's wonderful obsession. Careful and so funny. You can't really dig it online, they are objects you need to hold to appreciate."
—*Penn Jillette*

"By the brilliant and quirkily funny Bob Rucker. They are amazing! I have the full set."
—*Mary Roach*

"Every issue is a gem: Science, Economics, Floating Cars, Prank Gangplanks...and I've never seen so much Amalgamation!"
—*MK Brown*

"Has weaponized television hobbled your precious pineal gland? Let the healing begin with a subscription to *POPULAR PANDEMICS*!"
—*Justin Green*

"God I love *Popular Pandemics*. True art pieces. What a treat these are!"
—*Ron Turner*

← Look inside the latest issue.
Order and subscribe.

www.popularpandemics.com

@popularpandemics   @popularpandemi1

NEWS & POLITICS

SELF-IMPROVEMENT

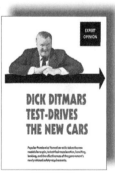

INSIGHT

COLLECT ALL 8 BEFORE YOU HAVE TO COLLECT 9!
popularpandemics.com

THE FUN PAGE

CLASSIFIEDS

UNIQUE ADS